Someone's Praying, Lord

Other Books by the Author:

Master of Men
The Congregational Way of Life
The Free Church Today

SOMEONE'S PRAYING, LORD

Arthur A. Rouner, Jr.

With a Foreword by the
Very Reverend Professor James S. Stewart
University of Edinburgh

Prentice-Hall, Inc., Englewood Cliffs, N.J.

Someone's Praying, Lord by Arthur A. Rouner, Jr.
©1970 by Arthur A. Rouner, Jr.
ISBN 0-13-822056-5
Library of Congress Catalog Card Number:
74-105716
Printed in the United States of America   T
Prentice-Hall International, Inc., London
Prentice-Hall of Australia, Pty. Ltd., Sydney
Prentice-Hall of Canada, Ltd., Toronto
Prentice-Hall of India Private Ltd., New Delhi
Prentice-Hall of Japan, Inc., Tokyo

To the one who loved me
When I did not deserve her love,
And who prayed for me
When prayer was my only life,
I dedicate gratefully
This book of prayers.

Foreword

It was when he was a student of theology at Edinburgh University that I first came to know the author of this book. In the Congregations he has served since then, he has exercised a strong and fruitful ministry: his understanding of men and women and their needs, his spiritual perception, his gift for translating the eternal Word into terms of the speech of today, his devotion to the Church and its Master — all this has made him a true ambassador of Christ in this generation.

Here in this book which he has given us are prayers which, while modern and contemporary in idiom, are marked by an intense reality, an awareness of the heights and depths of human experience, and that spirit of adoration which is the very life-blood of true religion. There is nothing nebulous, formal or conventional about these prayers: they are specific, forthright and particular, and throbbing with the wonder and exhilaration of the Christian faith. A book like this can do an immense service to the Church and to individual Christians, especially in an age like the present when so many radical question marks are being raised about the dimension of the transcendent and supernatural, and about the practice of the presence of God.

"Why has God established prayer?" asked Pascal more than three hundred years ago. And his answer was: "To communicate to His creatures the dignity of causality." That means in simpler language — prayer does things: To the humblest Christian who prays there belongs, under God, the dignity of initiating events. Archimedes used to say that, given a place to stand, a lever and a fulcrum, he could move the earth off its axis. A daring thought! But Kierkegaard's comment on it carries a challenge for us all: "The Archimedian point is an oratory where a man really prays in all sincerity — and he shall move the earth. It is unbelievable what a man of prayer can achieve if he will close the doors behind him."

I am inclined to think that the real trouble with the Church today is not theological stagnation, nor social apathy, nor moral confusion: It is a kind of prayer paralysis. Too often the Church has been content to offer one more diagnosis of the contemporary situation, one more analysis of the human predicament, one more panegyric of democracy, one more dull pithless ethic denuded of the supernatural. But surely what the world needs and expects from the Church, what the world is going to be dreadfully disappointed if it does not find there, is an altar where the fire is really burning, the authentic touch of the divine, the kindling contact of the flame of heaven. The most urgently necessary task for the Church is not, as certain theologians have suggested, the replacing of the Father image of God with some metaphysical abstraction about the ground of being; nor is it the construction of a semi-Freudian ethic to rationalize away our inhibitions. It is to take seriously the good news of the Holy Spirit, the divine redemptive energy embracing the universe and penetrating the lives of men. It is to expect great things from God in response to believing prayer.

At one point on their journey, Bunyan's pilgrims came upon a man down on his knees, with hands and eyes lifted up, who seemed to be speaking earnestly to One Who was above. The pilgrims could not hear what he said; but they noticed that, when he had finished, he rose to his feet and began to run toward the Celestial City. It is those who are often, like Mr. Standfast, down on their knees who can run where others only falter and stumble. "They go from strength to strength; every one of them in Zion appeareth before God."

May this book help many on that pilgrimage!

James S. Stewart

Contents

Introduction

Lots of people pray. Lots of people who would never admit it to their friends, pray. They may pray selfishly. They may pray in woeful ignorance of the ways of God. But they do pray.

They pray for peace. They pray for personal safety, for the protecting hand of God upon those they love, for the health of their friends who are sick. They pray for life, and for meaning. They bring to God concerns most of us would hardly suspect.

The problem today is not of men not wanting to pray. It is the problem of their not knowing how to pray. It is the problem of what to say. It is the struggle and embarrassment of not knowing how to put into words those deep feelings and longing desires that every man has within him.

This book is made up of prayers that struggled, in many different times and places, to be born within one man's life; to speak to God, not just for himself, but for other men too, those feelings most deeply felt, those long-ings most secretly longed, and those words most passionately needing to be said. They are offered in this form as expressions of what one man, "standin' in the need of prayer," felt and said in moments when his heart was most touched by God; in moments when he felt closest to the living Christ; in moments when he was most powerfully moved by the love, and wonder, and greatness of the Master of men.

My hope would be that this book might be an encouragement, a help along the way, to my fellow Christians, my pilgrim friends, who also look for a word to say that will tell the Lord what they feel in those moments when they, like John of Patmos long ago, are "in the Spirit on the Lord's Day."

A special word of thanks goes to my secretary, Mrs. Lois Collings, who willingly took time in her hectic schedule to turn handwritten pages lovingly, patiently, and skillfully into a typewritten manuscript for the publishers. Other thanks, too, go to my family, who endured forgivingly and under-standingly the long days taken away from them at the library, for two sum-mers while they were on vacation.

Arthur A. Rouner, Jr.
Tamarack Lodge
Lake Ossipee, New Hampshire

Prayers for a New Generation

O Christ of the ages
    Whose footsteps track the world,
    and Whose heart leans close to every human need:
It's an amazing thing for us to think how far You've come,
    how many miles You've walked,
    at how many doors You've knocked,
    at how many firesides You've sat,
    and at how many office parties, and union meetings,
        and faculty clubs You've been.
You do get around, Lord! Where haven't You been?
    —In a tavern, on a train, in a spacecraft, on a plane?
    No—You're out there, too. You, in Your offbeat way.

I suppose You were the first great nonconformist,
           the first far-out fellow this world ever had.
It's wonderful, Lord!
    In a day when the Church seems so pious and holy—
    its buildings are just too beautiful,
    and preachers and choirs look so pretty in their robes.
It's wonderful, Lord, to think You're out there in the world—
    that the Mexican day-laborers know You,
      that our President and lots of Congressmen know You,
      that some of the teamsters know You.
      That doctors in operating rooms,
        girls at switchboards,
          couples in retirement homes,
            young couples having their first baby,
          salesmen on the road,
            lawyers before the bar,
              and actors on opening night
                all know You.

How do you manage it, Lord? How can You care about so many in the
        crowd?
How can You get around, and be in so many places, and love so many
        people, Lord?

For Men of a Modern World

Forgive us, Lord, for not expecting You everywhere.
O Jesus, especially forgive us for not expecting You in poor places—
  in unpainted houses, with weeds and high grass in front,
  in alleys and taverns, and all those places that aren't very nice.
We forget about the barn, Lord, and about the baby born among the beasts.
  It never occurred to us that a Young Prince of Peace
  would ever find His power by growing up
    in Nothingsville, in Dullsville!
And that He would be crowned with thorns
 and throned on a cross
  and win His battles with a sword of the Spirit!
  O Lord we have so much to learn.
  Help us to see the light of the star today,
   and hear the sound of a song, and learn the knowledge of a truth!

Take this whole world, Lord, and hold it in Your Hand.

         Amen.

God! What a wonderful time it's been!
　　Thank You for Christmas with our families,
　　thank You for the touching remembrances of so many scores of friends,
　　　　through cards, and letters, and presents.
　　They really love us, Lord—imagine that!
　　　　Far away: some half a continent, or half a world, and oceans
　　　　　　away;
　　　　　　Yet they care about us!
　　Isn't that great?

Christ, You think it's great, don't you?
　　We know You do, because it would never have happened without You.
　　You do wonderful things to the hearts of men, Lord.
　　　　You've done wonderful things to our hearts this Christmas—
　　　　　　In fact, in this whole year!
　　Thank You. O Christ, thank You!
　　Little King, and Risen Lord, we honor You, and praise Your Name.
　　　　Glory be to Thee! Glory be to Thee!

O Jesus, Who comes so pure and innocent
　　　　　　and tiny and fragile in this holy season:
　　We who are so impure and unholy,
　　　　and anything but innocent,
　　confess to You how little we deserve Your friendship
　　　　and Your love.
　　We've done a lot of things we shouldn't have—
　　and lots of things we should have done
　　　　we've been too afraid to do.
　　We're ashamed of that, Lord.
　　We're ashamed even to kneel in the doorway of Your stable home.
　　　　That dirty floor with its straw and dust is too clean
　　　　a place for us, Jesus.

But we'd like to do something, to show we're sorry,
　　and that we want to try again
　　and are grateful for a thousand things You've done for us.

We'd like to offer You the lives we live in the world, Lord. . .
    Where we work,
    And have our influence.
That's not much. But we are in some pretty interesting places,
        and have quite an opportunity
            to put in a good word for You
            and for the Kingdom
          —if we'll take it—and if You'll help us.

Please help us! We really want to count for You where it will make a
    difference.
    We'd love to surprise the world,
        to surprise our friends, and our company people, our
            business partners.
    We'd really like to knock 'em over,
        to make them see that something has happened,
        —that we've got a great Lord and that we've found
          Him
        to be the answer.
It can be so exciting, Lord—exciting for businessmen,
            exciting for college students,
            exciting for housewives.
    Show us how, Lord. Hold us up. Pray for us!

                Amen.

O God of Creation,
>Who made the seas and the dry land,
>Who dug down the valleys, and raised up the mountains,
>Who flung the stars against the sky, and caused the light of the moon
>>to ripple upon the midnight lakes of summertime,
>>>and the dawn of winter's sun to rise in splendor across a white
>>>>land,
>>and to set in evening glory when day is done:

Our hearts have been filled with wonder at the sight of the whole world
>beneath our feet through other's eyes!

From high in a space capsule
>we have caught a vision of what the majesty of Your creation really is.
>We have seen the dawn and the sunset within a few hours.
>We have heard the silences of space
>>and the far-off singing of the spheres,
>>and our hearts are breathless with the wonder.

O God most high, wonderful Creator and blessed Saviour,
>we offer to You the grateful thanks of a whole people
>>for what our men in space have done.
>Your promise has been to bear us up,
>>lest we dash our foot against a stone.
>And we laud and magnify Your glorious name,
>>that in Your infinite mercy and tender care,
>>You did bear them up with Your everlasting arms,
>>>and did shelter them beneath the shadow of Your wing.

We praise You for their minds and spirit.
We thank You for their courage and humility.
We bless You for their faith
>and for their sure knowledge that the Lord is their Shepherd,
>and that even should they walk through the valley of death they need
>>not fear!

Grant us faith like theirs, Lord.
Let us trust You and be brave in You, just as they have trusted and been
>brave.

Let the example of their lives inspire our children and young people
    to deeds of love and mercy,
     and lives of courage and of faithfulness.

And Lord, as You have heard the nation's prayer for them—
    hear our prayer too, for all men
     who are trying to live as Your friends
      in this dangerous yet exhilarating day.

                Amen.

O God, Who has made some men brave in the faith,
    until the honors of Earth,
    and the acclaim of men,
    and the condescending approval of the powers that be
        meant nothing to them,
    but only the Truth counted;
O God, Whose Spirit enflamed the great saints and martyrs,
        the prophets and reformers of the faith
        from Stephen to Savonarola to Bernard of Cluny,
            to Hus and Wyclif, to Luther and Zwingli, and John Knox
                and Robert Browne
      crying out to the world,
           "Here I stand. I can do no other. God help me!"
We honor them.
  We praise their names!
   We laud and magnify them
    as they stand at last with Christ their Lord—
     brave soldiers of the Church militant;
       victorious conquerors in the Church triumphant.

For every unknown soldier of the Faith who has stood for right,
    and guarded principle when all about
    branded him the historic names of Christian ridicule—
        uncooperative, dissenter, heretic, rebel, and schismatic—
    but never succumbed and never recanted: We thank You, Lord.
We thank You for the heritage of truth they left us;
    and for the ringing words of faith they 'blazoned across the pages
      of our history to thrill us still!

O God, for the tameness of the Church today, forgive us.
      For her own abject conformities even while she condemns
         the "organization man" in the world around her, forgive us.
      From all our unfaithful fears at doing a new thing,
         and all vain attempts to save our lives instead of lose them,
           deliver us, we pray.

O conquering Saviour, Who came not to bring peace but a sword,
    and Who promised that in the days of war and rumors of war
    You would come again, riding upon the clouds of heaven,
    And that we were to look up, and lift up our heads,
        for our Redemption would be drawing nigh:
Lift up our heads now, O Lord. And not our heads only, but our hearts and
        our hands as well.

Make us proud of the Gospel.
    Put Your sword into our hands—the sword of Your Spirit:
    That not the powers of the darkness of this world
        nor the powers of subtle conformity in the Church itself
        may ever again defeat us, or cow our spirits,
        or ever make us subservient to any man's will when Your will is at
            stake!
And give us the faith to know that never shall we be led astray
    as long as Jesus Christ is the Lord of our life every day!

                                                    Amen.

O God the Holy Spirit, Who long ago came as a mighty wind
    through Jerusalem, sweeping away every doubt,
    and gathering every disciple of the Risen Christ into one place,
    there to fill them with a zeal, and a love, and a life
    like that city had never seen, and Judea had never seen, and the world
        had never seen . . .
We marvel at that power living and moving and breathing through the Church
    of Christ in all the centuries since.
We marvel at that love slaying sin and convicting consciences
    and lighting up lives in all those centuries since.
And we marvel at the power that has been unleashed through men into the
    world,
    changing the course of history,
    bringing the supernatural to bear upon the natural,
    and turning chance into Providence in all those centuries since!

O Jesus Christ,
    we look out upon the Church today—
        with so many hearts dead,
        with so many Christians no longer caring,
        with scores and hundreds in the Churches we are part of
            who bother not even to worship, except for an occasional
                Easter—
    and we ask: "Can these bones live?"
            O ye dry bones, hear the word of the Lord! Turn and
                believe!
            Give Christ a chance! Believe and live!

O Spirit of God,
    move across the face of Your great company today,
    and breathe upon the dry bones of the Church everywhere.
    Make the dead wood green again,
    and the dusty faith to become good soil for the Word again,
    and the desert in these hearts of our brothers to blossom like the rose
        again.

O Pentecostal fires from heaven, come down upon Your people today!
    Pour out Your power upon Your people today—
        upon the deacons of the Church,
            and upon the trustees, and missionaries, and all the boards;
            and upon the ministers of the Church
            and upon the Church schoolteachers.
                And Lord, upon the young people,
                especially upon the high school students who somehow
                still hang on, and still have a care for the Church.
                Lord, You know they are not always nor even often
                    here.
                    But change all that. Change their lives. Change
                      their hearts.
                Fill them with a spirit that will make them want always
                to walk with You.
                Touch their parents, Lord.
                    Especially those who are not really committed,
                        who have not really cared.
Change that now, Lord. Change it in them. Change it in us.
    Change it in the Church
        until it lives again, and we too live again in Christ.

                      Amen.

O God of this good day—how great You are!
   How great You are, in sun and star,
   in beauty near, horizon far.
      We're Yours, Lord. To the end of the Earth, we're Yours.
      We follow You. Say but the word
           and we'll rise up and follow You.

You've surely followed us.
   We've forgotten—but You never have.
   We've failed—but You never fail.
      Thank You for forgiving us.
      Thank You for dying for us while we were still sinners.
      Thank You for loving us today, and letting us walk Your way.
And thank You for always being there, Lord—
   at home when things are tough,
      in those classes that are always rough,
         on the playing field when the game is long,
           at the parties in our fun and song.

Lord, You are even there on the wilderness waters of the
   north this week! We thank You!
   Brooding over the quiet of the campfire, You are there; struggling
   under those packs along the portages, You are there.
      And in the laughing of the Loon,
         and the echoes from the hills,
           and in the dip of distant paddle—
You are there.
Be with those who will explore other waters.
   Be with our young people always, Lord,
      and confront them where'ere they go
      with the Christ their hearts can know!

And God, bless those who care about the young
         —those adults who are their friends
         —those busy people who take their time
           to care, and dare to walk youth's way
           and listen to what they say
           and show them how to pray.

For Teen-Agers and Their Struggle

Be with them and their young friends
  as they help them, we pray,
    to face every foe along the way,
      and so bring in our Christ's new day!

Amen.

Great and wonderful God,
    Who long ago made fires to burn in the hearts of
        patriarchs and prophets, and
    Who in every generation has made young men to
        see visions and old men to dream dreams;
You, Who have sent the winds of the Spirit to blow through the land,
    and set the lives of simple men on fire with faith, and have
    set a deep hunger in their hearts to know the truth;

We gather on this marvelous morning
    when this whole northern land is fresh with beauty and promise,
        to give You our thanks for all the winds of the Spirit
        that have blown through halls of learning
        and fanned a flame in these young people for
            the eager, exciting search for the truth.

We thank You, Lord, for little girls,
    for little girls who before our very eyes have become young women,
    for little girls who once thought the thoughts of youth
but who now dream the dreams of life. Girls
    who dream of a world waiting to be graced by their
        spirit and their ability and their service,
        who dream of a man who will be their man
        and of children who will be their children
        and of a life that will be their life.

O God, Who set these dreams in their hearts,
    make them all come true.
Hold You their hands and be their guard and their guide
    through life, and keep them always on the high roads of life,
    walking with brave hearts through life, and
    standing tall and strong and beautiful for the great truths of life.

So, Lord of all our lives, we come to this great day,
    to bless these young people on their way, and with full hearts to pray:

Shepherd of eager youth,
guiding in love and truth through devious ways,
Christ our triumphant King, we come Thy name to sing,
And here our children bring, to sound Thy praise.
Ever be our guide, our shepherd and our pride,
our staff and song.
Jesus, Thou Christ of God, by Thy enduring Word,
lead us where Thou hast trod, make our faith strong.

Amen.

O Lord of the high country,
    hiker on the heart's high hills—
        Who hails men out from hamlet and home
            to walk above the din and dirt of dull drab days,
            and makes them highland men who walk
                where the wind blows free,
                and the wonders of God can be:
Thanks for calling young people to follow Thee!
Thanks for putting into the heart of this genius generation—
    this bold, bright, brash band of boys and girls—
        to come into the Church on Sabbath day,
        to be dedicated to walking Your way.

Lord Jesus, our Saviour from sin,
    Who stands by the gate of the Cross to let us into
        the kingdom of Your love and care:
We're sorry for the ways we've booted it already in life.
We're sorry for lots of things—
            for deeds undone, for opportunities not taken,
              for fears felt, for days of dishonesty both intellectual and
                spiritual.
We ask You to forgive us, Lord.
 We ask You to heal and help us.
 We ask You to show us the way, and help us to walk it.

O God, we thank You for little kids
    who live and grow up and give the world their gift.
        We forget, Lord, that not all little boys and girls do live.
        We forget that life, very often, must be fought for.
And help us, Lord, to remember that even we do not live forever:
        that men die,
            and that if we're ever to really live
            we must know how to die.
    In a day of youth and promise,
        when life seems so endless and forever,
    remind us of even those young who are struggling for life.

We thank You, Lord God,
    that our young people in this day
    are so young and strong and on their way.
We thank You for their minds,
  and for their hopeful, seeking hearts—
   and for their faith in God,
    and for the love of the Lord Jesus
     with which You send them out into the world of today
     to win the victory in life's fray!

Amen.

O Lord,

> *When Stephen, full of power and grace,*
> > *Went forth throughout the land,*
> *He bore no shield before his face,*
> > *No weapon in his hand;*
> *But only in his heart a flame*
> > *And on his lips a sword,*
> *Wherewith he smote and overcame*
> > *The foemen of the Lord.*

For all the young Galahads of the faith, O Lord,
> those soldiers of the Spirit
> who, in the blush of youth, thought nothing of following the gleam
> and serving their Christ with body, and spirit, and soul—
> > We praise You,
> > > and give honor to the Name they loved.
> > > and to the cause they served!

O Spirit of calm courage and glad faith and high hope,
> Who made brave apostles of that band of the young so long ago:
> > Pour out Your Spirit upon the young of the Church today, we
> > > pray.
> > Give them brave hearts to fight the battles of the Lord,
> > and let them never be ashamed to confess the faith of Christ
> > > crucified,
> > and to be His soldiers and servants as long as they live.

O Lord, as You have sheltered these, our children, beneath the shadow of
> > Your wings,
> and lovingly have led them by the hand
> > and brought them to this day,
> go with them also from this day forth.
> As they have grown up here,
> > increasing in wisdom and stature and in Your favor and in ours—

let the same fineness of their character,
  and the same purity of their lives,
  and the same intelligence of their minds,
  and joy of their spirits,
go with them always.
And may they be a light to the world,
  a joy to their friends, and
  a witness where they live, and study, and work
    to the power and truth of Jesus Christ.

Let them find their Lord, we pray,
  to be Commander of their highest loyalty,
  to be Friend to their deepest heart,
  to be Light upon their darkest path,
  and to be Saviour of their inmost souls.

Bless them, Lord, for we love them, and we know You love them.
  May their young faith and brave spirits
  make us all soldiers of Christ,
  that by what all of us do in the world,
  honor may be done
  and praise be given
    to Your Name—forever and forever.

        Amen.

Father in heaven
    Who knows me better than I know myself,
    Who has looked in every heart of man
        and seen the secrets and the hopes,
            the doubtings and the loves:
For a hundred things that mean the world to me—
      not land or freedom,
          but home and friends,
              family and faith—
                  I sing my praise to You, O God.

That unto me should come the gift of tender love,
    I stand amazed, with wonder, Lord.
That there should be a hand to take my own,
    and eyes to look on me in love,
      and one to be the loyal friend
          to walk with me life's way—
        what can I say,
            but thank You, Lord!

And for the children of that love . . .
How can any man give thanks enough for what
      his little ones
      mean to him?
    Tousled heads when dawn comes up,
        and shrieking wild, and laughing friends
          who hold him tight when day is done
          and home he comes.

  Little eyes above the table top,
      tiny hands in yours when down the street you walk.
      Sturdy son,
        your best companion
          along the mountain trails of summer fun.

For Families

And when the night comes down,
   and by their beds you sit,
     what stars look in
         and shine with far-off wisdom
          in those precious eyes!

I thank You, Lord!

               Amen.

O Great God, Who made the world for children
    Who made the sky for young eyes to count the clouds
        and search the infinite blue,
    Who made the baking sun to brown the bare bodies
        of the young, and
    Who made the grass for children's feet
        to run wild and free:
      We thank You that the Master of men
        was the friend of children!
      We thank You that He Who was a man among men,
        Who wielded the carpenter's hammer
        and made yokes for the oxen,
        Who was the friend of fishermen
        and the foe of Pharisees
        and the forgiver of the forsaken,
could also see the kingdom of heaven in the hearts of children.

O Jesus Christ,
    Who never was afraid to have the conversation of the old
        interrupted by the cries of the young,
    and Who overruled the protests of Your protectors
      with the great invitation:
      "Let the little children come to Me!"
    With glad hearts, O Lord, we bring our children unto You today.
     With all our joy,
      with all our pride, and
      with all our humility,
  we bring to You the dearest that we have in life.
    That here in Your house they might be consecrated to Your cross,
      and received as children of the Church
      and as followers of the Lord of the Church.

In blessing our children, O Lord,
    bless us as well.
        Rededicate every Christian conscience
          to the company of the Christ
          of which we all have promised to be a part.

For Babies at Their Baptism

And give Your Holy Spirit to these children's lives.
    Put Your hand around each one's heart,
  and with the finger of Your faith
      touch their parents' conscience.
  And hear us, as all the families of Earth we remember,
    and every child we know,
      who needs You.
  For Your love's sake.

      Amen.

O God,
>Who makes every bud on every tree
>>a promise that the spring will come; and
>Who makes the turning grass from winter's death
>>to luxurious life
>>a promise that the warm Earth
>>>will yet mother us again,
>>>and we shall lie next to her
>>>>in the summer sun
>>>>and be healed and restored;

O God of the turning Earth,
>Who brings the springtime in its season,
> and Who wakes our very bodies
> and stirs up our winter spirits into life, and joy:
>Hear this people's cry, as we shout
>"Hosanna!" and "Alleluia!" unto You,
>>the God Who gives the gift of life
>>and makes us young, and glad, and grateful!

On this day, O God, of Earth's turning into life,
>we give You special thanks for the little lives
>>of our children, whom we have brought to You today.
>They are the very best we have—
>>the loveliest,
>>>the purest,
>>>>the most beautiful, and good.
>They are the promise of all that we ourselves have not become.
>>We have failed, and fallen short—
>>>but they will be strong
>>>and sweep all things before them in their path.
>>We have been so ordinary, so mundane in life—
>>>but they will be heroes and heroines
>>>in the brave new world to come.

We have not stood upon the ramparts
and been the watchmen of our time—
but they will scan the skies of the future,
and pierce the darkness with their light,
and be for Christ and for the kingdom
faithful servants and good soldiers:
keepers of the peace,
brave for any battle,
glad children of the world's new day.
This is what we hope, and what our hearts would pray today.

Now look, O Lord, on those who long ago were little children in Your house.
Look upon our young people—
the ones in college, the high school students, the ones in confirmation.
O Lord, in that world where temptations come so easily,
and weak foundations of the past can break down so quickly—
make their faith strong!

Amen.

Prayers for Our Land
and for Our Leaders

O God, the daybreak in bright October is such a glory in our land!
We can scarcely speak before the splendor of autumn leaf and light in old
New England.

Each fall it is as if we had never seen it before!

Never seen the sky-blue that only October brings;

never seen the flaming foliage that makes a glory-land of country
roads;

never seen the ripening harvest, the apples in the orchards,
the pumpkins in the fields.

It is a miracle of the land, O Lord,
a miracle of this land that You have given us, and we thank You.

For all the blessings of a great land, O Lord, we give You humble
thanks,
and praise Your name! And not alone for little New England,
but for the rich farmlands to the West,

for the drifting prairies broad and beautiful,

for the Rockies that crown the land with snow-capped majesty,
and for the mighty oceans that thunder in along our coasts,

we praise You, Lord.

For all that is made beautiful because of freedom,
and because of faith, we thank You, Lord.

O God, Who made us once a Christian people who strode to live by
heaven's law, who loved Your Word in Scripture and in Psalm, who felt
themselves privileged to worship every Sabbath day in the house of the
Lord:

We have not loved You as our fathers loved. We have grown careless in
our faith, and we have made worship in Your house a matter of convenience
and not of conscience; a matter of comfort instead of sacrifice; a matter
of fancy instead of faith.

Forgive us, Lord, that we think more of ourselves than we do of You.
And forgive the Church in this land that before the world has seemed really
to care so little. Give us a new heart, Lord, and a new spirit, we pray.

We speak a special prayer for the whole world and for the United
Nations.

For the Land We Love

O Lord, Who has given men a vision of world government and world
            concern,
let anger die,
  and hatred fail,
    and fear fall away—
until in love men can sit down as brothers to do the work of peace.
        We offer to You our land, that her freedom, and her faith,
            and her vast resources, and her own search for peace
            may be for the healing of the nations.

                              Amen.

O God of our fathers, Whose Spirit has gone before Your people
        for a hundred generations
    like a western star,
      leading them onward
        and calling them out from every safe harbor and home
          to be pioneers and pilgrims on Earth;
God of the open sea and the flapping sail;
God of the gray coastline and the untracked forests;
God of the turnpikes and the airways;
God of every Christian man's free spirit;
God of the longing heart,
  and the questing mind,
    and the eagle eye . . .
      Cloud by day and
        pillar of fire by night to every man of faith:
Glory be for Your guiding hand along life's way.
    Thanks be for the sun on the hills,
      and the song of the road,
        and the call of a great company carrying on.

O Lord Jesus, hear our prayer of thanks—
  for the fields bare and waiting, with the harvest gathered in;
    for a crop that came despite disaster and storm;
      for lives preserved in face of flood, and in time of tornado;
      for every safe flight of an airline's plane;
      for your hand in the history of man and
        in the life of this nation;
        for the vision that filled our fathers' hearts;
        and for the dream we dream today.
    For all of this, we thank You!

O God of history, Who works out Your purposes through men and nations,
      deal decisively, we pray, with Viet Nam and every place of war,
        and bring peace out of a peril that perverts,
        and a willingness to live together out of a war that tears men apart.
    And work Your way with us all!

          Amen.

Lord, I want to be a Christian, in my heart. . .
    I want to be more holy, in my heart. . .
    I want to be like Jesus, in my heart. . .

I haven't been very much like Jesus in my heart this week.
Lord, I haven't been like You at all!
    I'm ashamed of what I've been.
    I'm ashamed of what America has been.
    I'm ashamed that another name
            has been added to the names of infamy in America—
            that our sin stands stark and bare in Selma,
            and that beside the names of John Brown,
                            Abraham Lincoln,
                            Medgar Evers,
                            John Kennedy,
        there stands another martyr's name.

O Jesus Lord, have mercy upon Jim Reeb.*
    Bare up his broken body in Your arms,
    and take him home with You,
        to Your kingdom where he's free.
    Take him for what he's been and done,
    and for the love he lived,
    and open his eyes to see
        that there's a new life in a great new land where he will be.
    Heal him in Your kingdom, O Lord Christ,
        and lay a tender hand on his widow's broken heart,
        and on his children's wondering and uncomprehending heads!

We praise You, giver of every life,
    for the witness of those men who give their last—
                        who dare to lose their lives, and so to
                                find them.
                Greater love has no man than this.

O God, give us this love that gives its all, and so is perfect.
        Give us this love that's unafraid, and so is worthy.
*A young Unitarian minister killed in Selma.

For Justice in the Land

O put Your love into us all.
Make it so to blaze in our hearts
  that it may turn back the darkness of days like these
  and bring a new life of justice, and
      truth, and
        love to our land, and to our lives.

In Jesus' Name,
  Who only can make us Christians in our hearts.

       Amen.

O Spirit of the Living God,
    Passion of burning faith that flickered into life
        the grief-numbed souls of eleven men in a lonely room,
    Hallow this bare place with Your presence,
    bless the food of bread and wine.
    Make this cup that passes from hand to hand
    a deep unending spring of heavenly grace and Christian power,
    till every soul that drinks its draught becomes
    a spirit strong to fashion old men into new creatures,
        dead ideals into possible realities,
        and earth-bound faith into heaven-blessed knowledge.

O Spirit of the Living God,
    stand across our willful way as eternal justice.
    Confront us with the stern demands
        that are the meat and drink of heaven's children.
    Show us the subtle cruelties with which we live,
        and send us to our knees in shame.
    Show us the slums and crowded streets
        that still infest this land of ours.
    Show us the mere children who wait trial for petty crime
        in prison cells where hardened convicts teach them hatred.
    Show us the prejudice in these hearts of ours that lets us think
        it is white skin or gentile heritage that makes the man.
    Show us our hateful cliques that bar from our doors
        all friendless souls.
    Show us the spirit of self-righteousness that makes sham of all
        our pretense to be the Christian Church.
    And show us, Lord, the wrath of God's righteous anger.
    Give us eyes to see the raging storm on Zion's height,
        and to know that God is angry with His people.

And then, O Spirit of the Living God,
    come to us in the compassion of Your great forgiveness.
    Cry into our deafened ears the glorious words from Calvary—
        "Father, forgive them. . . ."

Lift our shamed eyes from the dust of repentance to see
    the Good Shepherd reaching toward us with His hand held out.
By forgiveness free us from the curse of pride—
    the pride that lets us take God's work and call it ours.
Free us from the words "I did,
    I helped, I healed, I loved, I gave, I taught, I preached, I prayed."
God, we don't do these things: Forgive us for the injustice of our
    pride!

And with the burdens of sin cast off by Your forgiveness,
    cause us to stand as free men of Christ,
    with a love boundless as the sea to help the little ones
    of Earth, given us by Thee.
Make us intercessors at the Mercy Seat for every life in need of God,
    and for ourselves—who need Him most.

And now, hear You this prayer, spoken by our lips and uttered in the
    quiet pleading of our hearts.
In the Name of Christ the Lord, from whence Your Spirit comes.

                                    Amen.

Lord Jesus, all the world is Yours today—
> The nations are Yours, and the people are Yours.
> Even the congregations gathered in worship, and
> the truckers on the nation's highways, and
> the nurses on hospital wards, and
> the sailors on ocean vessels, and
> soldiers in alien camps, and
> kings and diplomats,
> beggars and thieves—all are Yours!

In prayer we lift our eyes beyond the horizons
of our own lives and needs
to the great world beyond that perishes in its need for You.

Remember the United Nations, Lord, to which so much of the world looks
> with hope.
For the vision that inspired it,
for the dedication of those of many nations
> who labor to make it work, we thank You.
Be the Lord of the United Nations!
Work Your will through this instrument of men,
that it may become the instrument of God.

Remember the political parties of our land as they campaign.
We are grateful that by the mysterious will that no man knows,
You give us men of stature, and intelligence, and humility, and eloquence
> to lead the land in days demanding greatness.
Preserve us, Lord, from all malice in our political loyalties.
Teach us respect and charity toward those who differ
> from us in their convictions.
Go Lord, with these men who seek the highest honor and most
> thankless service that this land can give:
> that they may speak the truth, and care for human lives
> and for all the needs of men—old and young,
> > poor and rich, black and white.
> And give them, more than any other gift, the gift of patient wisdom
> > and daring courage to win the peace, for which all men long.

For Politicians

And Lord, look upon our land's young people,
>   and call out from them some who will serve You
>   and the world as well,
>   in politics and statesmanship as servants of Jesus Christ,
>   in a day when this land and all the world
>   needs Jesus Christ
>   if it ever is to be saved.

Amen.

O Jesus Christ, Who never held a sword, Who never killed a soul,
   Who never led an army, and yet reigns the King of kings:
   We come a Christian people in the dawning of the day,
      and at the threshold of the year, to pray for peace.
   O Christ, Who came a man of peace, to still the turbulence
         not alone of troubled minds and tortured lives,
         but also of the raging seas,
      You Whose command even the wind and waves obey:
            Hear now our plea as we bend heart and mind in the cause of
               peace!

Grateful are we for Christian leaders in the Church of Rome,
   who have given love and leadership
   in a bid to change the minds of warring men.
Grateful are we for thousands of Your people everywhere,
   who in Christmas season lifted up their hearts in prayer
   for the beating of the swords to plowshares, and the spears to pruning
      hooks,
      that the Star of Bethlehem might be a light of peace
      in a darkened world of war.

O Jesus, Whose Spirit is not bound by any nation's border,
   Who needs no passport to cross the frontiers of countries,
   to penetrate the front lines of armies,
   or to invade the lands of alien ideologies—
   You are as familiar with the jungles of North Viet Nam
      and the headquarters in Hanoi
      as You are with the avenues of our suburbs,
      or the offices of our cities,
      or the churches of America.

We forget that, Lord.
   We forget that Hanoi and Peking and Moscow are Your cities,
   and that China and Russia and Yugoslavia and East Germany are Your
      countries
   as much as London and Washington, and England and America.

For Peace

Those men are not alone, Lord.
>Those diplomatic couriers and counselors are not alone as they
>>bargain for peace.
>You are there, Lord. You're at those council tables;
>You're at those command posts; You're out there on those front lines.
>And You hold those men in the hollow of Your hand!
>Open their eyes to see. Make humble their hearts to know.
>Let their ears listen till they hear the world's cry,
>>that too many people have died.

Help our own government to have the wisdom and compassion
>to be not devious but to speak the truth.
>Let us be not rattlers of swords, or shouters of threats.
>Make America calm, and kind, and brave enough even to compromise
>>where principle will allow.
>And let the missions of men of peace succeed,
>by the power of Your saving hand, the hand that will heal the nations.

Amen.

O Lord our God, on this holy night
    there is a stillness that settles o'er the land.
    Even on far-off battlefields the guns are silent
    and there is a kind of peace tonight.
O Lord, what wonder that a tiny child can do all that to men!
Lord, He really is the Prince of Peace, isn't He?
      That little Child—Wonderful Counselor, the Mighty God,
        the Everlasting Father, the Prince of Peace!
      To have made presidents pause,
        and popes and premiers take counsel together.
      What a man this little King must be!

He's Your Son, Lord. He's Your hope for the world.
    If any light is ever to defeat the darkness, He is that Light.
    If any king is ever to win all men's allegiance, He is that King.
    If any man is ever to be the man of the hour, the man to meet the
        world's great need,
      He is that Man.

O God, crown Him tonight, we pray.
    Give Him His scepter, Lord, and let Him rule. We need Him.
    The whole world needs Him. Send Him to us, O Lord, this hour.
    Make the miracle happen for Your people, Lord—
      the midnight miracle of the song in the night,
      and the dark turned to light, and the knock heard the more
        at every heart's door,
        till we no more hide but open the door wide!

O little King, You'll have a hard time getting used to us!
    We are so slow to get the idea, so slow to understand that You
    are really born tonight—that You're alive, now, and not just long ago,
    and that You're here, and with eyes of faith You can be seen.

O Jesus, I've never heard an angel sing,
      I've never heard the heavens ring,
      I've never seen the sky alight,
      I've never seen You with my own sight.

But Jesus Christ, I know You're there.
 I know I've seen You with a mystic sight.
 Help me tell the people of those ways tonight.
 Help me set their lives alight!

We thank You, Prince of Peace, for the silence of Viet Nam's battlefields
  tonight.
We thank You that into that silence is coming Your love that can bring
  peace,
 and can still the guns forever.
 Make it come, O Lord. Make it come tonight!
 And make Your comfort come, O Christ, to all the weary world.
 And send us into this Christmas night with a song to sing,
 and a King of kings,
 and a great hope for a new world lifting up our step.
 Glory to God in the highest!

   Amen.

Prince of Peace, Great Commander on all the world's battlefields,
    You Who died among soldiers, and was born into a world of soldiery,
    and Who, by Your Spirit has marshaled men into a great army of the
        Lord:
    We turn to You on this day of the fluttering of flags,
        and the rolling of drums,
        and the marching of feet to the sounds of war,
        with our anguished hearts looking for solutions
        to the complex and controversial problems of finding peace.
We want to find the way, Lord, and we do not agree on what it is.
    Some of us are so uncertain.
    Others are so sure that we must fight our way through,
    that we must hack and slash and shell our way through,
    like crusaders with the Cross held high,
    until victory is complete and all our enemies die.
But we are not sure, Lord. We don't know if this is right.
    We do not know what is our Christian duty.
    Help us to see the truth—whatever it is.
    Help us to find the way—whatever it is.

We confess, Lord, that sometimes we get our politics mixed up with our
        religion.
    We even confuse the American way of life with the Christian way of
        life.
    But we do not mean to, Lord.
    We want to be Yours, Lord. Your army, Your soldiers, Your troops
        in a world crying out for revolution,
        for an invasion from the hosts of heaven,
        that will set Earth free from the dark death
        that would destroy it eternally.

Help us, O Lord, to find the path to peace!
    Help us to find our way to the negotiating tables.
    But help us, too, to be brave defenders of freedom's trust.
    Help us to be watchmen on the towers of truth,
        ready to fight every force that would enslave either a man's
        body or his mind.

Make us good soldiers of Christ, whether our place of battle
    be at a desk, or in a classroom,
    or in an office, or on the highway,
    or in the armies, or the fighter squadrons,
    or the navies of the world.
Be with our men who loyally bear their country's arms.
    and who do it bravely in the name of peace.
    Make each one brave to do his duty,
    and give him faith to forget not that he is a Christian.
As we struggle to know what's right, neither let us forget!

                         Amen.

O Mighty God, the ruler of the nations,
     Who has the whole world in Your hands:
     We Your people gather here tonight stunned, and awed,
     at the tragic death in Dallas that has struck today.
     We know only a great grief hugging round our hearts,
     and a brokenness throughout the land that
     only You can heal.

We would take our leader in our arms
     and bring him back to life if it were possible.
     With all our hearts we prayed he might be spared.
     But it could not be, and now he is with Thee,
     and You will make him whole and give him life
     in Your Kingdom that is in heaven.
We thank You for his bravery and courage in face of disagreement,
     and for the visions he had of great new frontiers for the land he loved.

We pray now for his family:
     for his wife, and for his little girl, and uncomprehending tiny son.
     Hold them all close to You, and comfort them,
     and give to them the sure hope of the eternal life for which we all
               strive,
     and which so suddenly has come out of the night to their husband and
               father.
And we pray for his mother and father,
     so proud and grateful, and now so desolate and dismayed,
     and for his brothers and his sisters.
Give us grace to surround them all with our love and prayers.

And now we pray for him upon whom destiny has thrust so suddenly
     the highest office in the land.
     Be with him to uphold his hands and make strong his heart,
     and give courage to his spirit.
     Crown him with wisdom and with righteousness,
     and let the people's love and loyalty reach out to encourage and to help
               him.

For the Nation's Need Tonight

And we pray for our country—our poor broken and weeping country.
    Lay Your hand upon us.
    Help us know that the everlasting God fainteth not, neither is weary.
    Help us to see a light in this deep darkness.
    Forgive us, and heal us, and help us to rise up from this disaster
        with new humility, and new power, and new love.
            To rise up with wings as eagles,
            to run and not be weary,
            to walk and not be faint.
Hear our prayer, O Lord.
Hear our prayer, O Lord.

        Amen.

Prayers in the Deep of Winter

O Great God of this northern land,
    Who paints with frosty finger frozen wonders on our windows,
    and Who blankets the Earth with snow as if it were Your hand,
        pure, and white, and beautiful,
        lying close against the Earth to give it warmth, and moisture,
        and its long winter sleep:
We're glad for the promise of a white Christmas,
    and for the week of wondrous expectation left to us—
    when we can walk out in the still cold of Advent nights
    and dream upon the stars,
    and maybe, in some solitary moment in that darkness,
    hear upon the wind the distant sounds of singing from on high,
    and know that angels are abroad to sing a message in the sky!
Praise be for winter's advent
    and for this white and waiting world to which it comes.

O merciful and gracious God:
    Have pity on our world so hurt and broken by the hates of men,
    and so long divided by the deceits of men.
    Heal the bleeding heart of a world broken by the burden of a dark
        sorrow
        fired in madness into the heart of a Texas town
        and spread, until it broke the heart of the whole world down.
    Save us, O God.
    Save a world with so many hurts in so many places—
        in Berlin and Cuba, in South Africa and Viet Nam,
        in Dallas and in Washington.
    Let Your hand hold and heal us.
    Let Your love come to our hearts, in this season of the star.
    Let the purity and promise of the Child of Bethlehem
        drive away all that has hardened us to human needs.
    Humble us. Grant us the spirit of repentance.
    Show us how to love each other—and our enemies—
    and how to give to others what our hearts have.

On a Winter Morning

And God, give us hearts to hear the angels sing,
    and sight to see the star when it begins to shine,
    and lives to lift in joy at the wonder of the winter
        and the One Who gave it all that we might not fall.

                        Amen.

O God, Who again has covered the hard ground of winter's iron
    with the soft beauty of heaven's whiteness,
    and at Whose command the sun rises
        and turns to morning glory all the sleeping land:
We who have walked out into the winter wonder of this new day,
        and whose hearts have marveled at the splendor that before us in
        beauty lay,
sing to You glory and gladness, and wonder and joy!

For everything the day has brought, we thank You, Lord:
    not alone for beauty on the Earth, or splendor in the skies,
    but also for the day this is—for Sunday;
        for a world whose wheels of industry grind to a stop
        and men go home to rest, and traffic slows,
        and cities keep silence, and church bells ring,
        and men bow down and give You thanks,
        and ask Your help and go away as men made new—
            refreshed, and strong, and one with their God again.

O God, let this be such a day for us.
    Let it be a day in which the bending near of God seems very close;
    a day when worship brings a Word from Him,
        and help, and hope, and healing strength.
Help us to see Jesus!
We know He comes when hearts are wide to ask Him in.
    Ours swing wide this hour, Lord. We need Him.
    We need to see His face, and hear His voice,
    and feel the touch of His strong hand.

In the silence of this day when a little perspective returns
    and we can see ourselves again,
    we ask You not to let us hurt each other.
    Let our fellowship be only for the healing of the wounds of life,
        and not for cutting them deeper.

Help us hold our brother's hand in ours,
and in our daily prayers, his heart.
And help our lives to be in everything we say or see,
a power for peace and love, through all eternity.
For Your Love's sake.

Amen.

O God! What a day You've made!
    I stand—a city man—
    upon this height,
    remembering the blight like night
    of tedious city streets made marvelous like the morning.

It's all behind me, Lord:
    the slush and the rush,
    the papers and desks,
    the people and pests
        with all of the problems
        and the trouble to solve them.
    For a few hours they're gone.
    They're part of the world—
        the smoke of the plain,
        the folk mean and vain—
    that I stand above
    in these hours I love.

I look to the hills, and the earth lying still at my feet,
    where sky and world meet,
    while I stand above, on this slope that I love,
    with wings on my feet,
    with only wind I must beat,
        As I sweep down the hill
        No obligations to fulfill
        But just not to spill—
    to take my turns with some grace
    and to keep up the pace
    even though I'm no ace.
        Just let my cares go,
        my body bend and bow,
        and my heart in me know
    that You, Lord, are here,
    that I've nothing to fear
    in these moments so dear!

On the Ski Slopes

God! Thanks for these hours to ski,
>   to be out on these hills with Thee!
>   For the warm lodge there below, with the fires that glow,
>   and the sun on the snow that helps me to know
>>   that You are my God,
>>   that You want me here,
>>   that You're setting me free
>>   to be the man I must be—
>>>   all thanks unto Thee!

>   Amen.

O Advent God, Who out of the night sky
    looked down on Earth and chose Bethlehem for Your home;
    and in that little town, sleeping silent beneath the stars,
    chose there, of all unlikely places,
    a humble room below an old inn's undercroft
    for the Holy Child to come,
    and made it that night the throne room of a King:
        Glory to God in the highest,
        and on Earth peace, goodwill toward men!

O God, what a miracle that things so lowly
    could become so lordly!
    What a miracle that stable straw
        could birth the Prince of Peace!
    What a miracle that the very heavens
        should sing in the night good tidings of joy—
            that unto us is born a Saviour!

O Mighty God, Everlasting Father, Prince of Peace:
    Hear now a people's prayer, as down our hearts we bow in Advent awe.
O Wonderful Counselor
    Who has heard the heartbeat of the world
    and has looked upon every sorrow, every sin,
        every bit of brokenness that ever touched the human heart:
    We confess our sin.
    So often we are centered on ourselves
    and want no cross to bear, no wounds of the world to share,
    no sackcloth like Christ's to wear!

O gracious God, Who always has been known in humble things,
    Who sent the Son of Man from His birthplace in a stable
    to the workshop of a carpenter, make us humble, too.
    And let it never be said that the doors of our hearts and of our Church
        are not open to the weary of the world, and the lonely and the
        lost, and the poor and the plebeian, and the dark-skinned and the
        alien.

On an Advent Night

O God, if it were Bethlehem's night again,
    and a star were to shine again, and a Saviour to come again:
    Let it not be us who would hear the angel's song and turn away,
    who would see in the sky a light and would not follow,
    who would stand at a stable door but be too proud to kneel!

Open our hearts.
    Let our ears listen for the songs of the Advent sky.
    And let our lives live in love for the One
    Who will not be long beyond the song.

                    Amen.

O God of the listening ear, and the aching heart, and the beckoning hand,
    Who bends low upon the waiting air each Christmas time
    to see if somewhere a new soul looks up to You,
    to hear if somewhere a newborn heart speaks soft to You in prayer:
        Listen, Lord.
    Look down now, Lord, for here a heart is raised to You,
    a voice speaks soft in whispered hope to You.

O Lord, we do not count ourselves religious men.
    The world is very much with us. Our days are full of
    hurried breakfasts, lurching trains, and crowded highways,
    of busy meetings, hard decisions, and nights too late
    for weary bodies and burdened spirits.
But God, who knows what yet we might be?
    We are not unmoved by Christmas, Lord.
    There is something about these days that touches even us;
    something about tinsel on the streets,
    the Christmas greetings in the stores,
    about candlelight in churches,
    about the old familiar story of Bethlehem and the star,
    of a stable and a Child that starts a longing down inside.
A longing to see the brilliant heavens the wise men saw,
    to hear the nighttime song the shepherds heard,
    to love the strange and wondrous Child that Mary loved.
There is something in us, Lord, that hungers for the heights,
    that is dazzled by the star,
    that yearns for a leader and a Lord,
    that is almost ready to follow the One Who said, "Come unto Me."

O God, is there something we could be, in Your kingdom?
    Is there a part we could play in Your search for men?
    Could we help? Could we be Your warriors in the world?
    Could we be Crusaders of the Cross?
    Could we be men of vision, like the wise men and shepherds?
    And could we be humble and faithful, like the mother Mary?

On Christmas Eve and Christmas Day

Here we are, Lord—lots of us. Call us this Christmas.
   Make our weak ones strong, our sorrowing ones courageous,
   our sick ones whole, our uncertain ones sure.
   And bind heart to heart and life to life,
   that in the Name of Christ the King
   we may tell all men tidings
   that are of great joy—great joy!

                    Amen.

O God of this holy Christmas Eve,
    when the strange star shines,
    and distant voices sing,
    and in the night a tiny baby cries,
    and from the heaven comes down a song—
        "Alleluia! Glory in the highest!"
    Our hearts are breathless at the mystery
    of what this night will bring!
    Our spirits are restless to go to Bethlehem
    and see this thing!

O little Lord Jesus, steal upon our hearts tonight,
    for we wait for You, we long for You, we look for You!
Little Child of the heavens, become man tonight,
    steal into this crowded Church, we pray—
    if not as a manger babe
    then as some stranger from afar—and stand beside us.

Sing with us as we sing tonight.
Pray with us as we pray tonight.
Listen with us as we strain against the silence
    to hear God's music crying out Your coming,
    and lay Your hand close to every heart.

If a soul is sad in the dark tonight,
    draw it close to You in the candlelight.
If a heart is hurt with a wound tonight,
    pour on Your balm and make it right.
On all the world's sin we beg You look,
    and make whole—and forgive
    that sin, particularly, with which we live.

If anywhere tonight there be those who see no Christmas light,
    whose eyes see not the manger love come down from the height:
    Touch them, teach them,
    and let the Christ within their door never to leave them anymore!

O Lord, tonight in this service of song and praise,
    as midnight comes, and our candles we raise—
    fill us with all the glad joy of these days,
    till in the silence our own hearts sing the song the angels say:
        "Jesus Christ is born today, Christ is born today!"

                                   Amen.

O God, we never thought this day would come—
　　this Christmas Sabbath with the great deed done.
Filled all with brightness white and clear,
　　and the knowledge that the little Christ is here!

We never knew how the world would thrill
　　to the sound of angels on the air so still.
We never knew how men would pray,
　　till Jesus the Master showed men the way!

This is the day when we all draw near
　　and sing the praise of the God men fear.
For the tiny Lord in the manger bare,
　　Who taught the world to bow down there.

O Christ of crib, and cross, and crown,
　　before Your love our hearts bow down,
that we Your people on this day
　　may shout the praise we long to say!

"Glory! Glory to our God today!
　　Make in the desert Christ's Highway!
Glory to our Christ we sing,
　　all our light, and love, and life we bring."

Take You these gifts of heart and hand,
　　Let no life here slip by like sand.
But make us brave and bold to stand,
　　sentries and soldiers who bear Christ's brand!

And so, at Christmas, once more we claim,
　　not wealth or fortune, friends or fame.
But only in life's battle, wax or wane,
　　the honor that the Saviour gives, to bear His Name.

　　　　　　　　　　　Amen.

Prayers on a Summer Sunday

O Master from the mountainside,
    Who is the same yesterday, today, and forever;
O Lord of us all,
    Who is the same on a July morning in a village church,
    among the everlasting hills,
    as You are on winter days amid clanging traffic,
    in the great cathedrals of a smoky city:

We who have come to rest awhile,
    who have cast a thousand cares aside,
    who long have hungered for these hills,
    take now our silent places in this church with grateful hearts.
        Grateful for this day's sun and sky,
        grateful for summer's meadows and her early flowers,
        grateful that a church's doors are open wide that God's House
            be not forgotten,
        grateful that God is here, and that His love stands at the door
            and knocks, waiting only for us to let Him in.

O God Who comes so close in Jesus Christ,
    Hear the prayers we people ask.
    We pray for healing for our work-worn bodies,
        for peace for our anxious spirits,
        for forgiveness for our sin-bound lives.
    And we pray for the hope, and the promise, and the gladness,
        and the joy that Jesus gives. And we ask that it may
        be given us; that this hour now may speak to us
        of truth, and love, and joy.

We pray for the churches from which we come—
    for those still who minister there,
    and those who with them worship there.
We pray Your Gospel to have glory and gladness for all
    who hear today, wherever it may be they pray.

In the Mountains

And for the special people who ever are on our hearts, we pray,
    because of the burdens they bear today,
    because of the loneliness of their way,
    because of the great decisions they must make,
    because of new adventures they must undertake—
        for a thousand reasons these friends we'll not forsake.

And for our country and our President, too, we pray.
    For the wisdom of all men in power; and for our own wisdom,
    and humility, and strength to meet the issues of this hour.
    Every hope and joy that's ours we offer to You, O Lord,
        Whose very Name is power: Jesus, our Christ and God.

                                  Amen.

O God of this summer Sunday,
Who gathers us here beneath these pines
in a quiet place apart within sound of the sea:
 Thanks for everything that makes this day our gift from Thee.
 Thanks for the salt smell in the air,
   for the gulls turning in the blue,
   for prayer in a place like this, where people come
    to hear a Word from You.
 Thanks for everything, O God, that this day means.

And Lord, as we walk down this little harbor road and gather here,
 most of us strangers from far and near,
 we ask You to bind us close and show us by one clear sign
 that we are Yours, and so are, no matter from how far,
 nor from what traditions we are.

Look upon these people, Lord.
Look into every seeking heart and see the longing there.
Feel in every faithful life the fighting there,
 and the fear that's near.
 And hold out Your healing hand to all of us, O Lord.
 Some here have sorrows in their hearts, and we pray You'll comfort
   them.
 Some are afraid of what's ahead with hearts that bled,
 and we pray You'll stand sure and certain in their stead.

Be also, Lord, our nation's help, as in the summer days a crisis grows.
Make us men of the Church, be part of the revolution that sweeps America,
 changing life and men along its way.
 With Your compassion, courage, tenderness,
 make us fit to work for justice among men
 and that equality before God for which our Saviour died.

By the Sea

And from this quiet summer place on a little harbor road,
    send us each with lives of love—Your love, O Lord,
    and with the gladness of a Gospel
    that has been this world's assurance
       and its only song, all along.

     Amen.

O God, Who must have made the sounds of the sea
  and brought back the winds from the East to me,
Who made the rolling thunder of the surf
  to give my city spirit a great new birth!
Who made the breakers in the bay,
  and New England's flowers beside the way,
  and lush green beauty on every hand:
We, Lord, who come from far-off city street
  with secret hope our Lord to meet
  within the quiet of summer days
  along the mountain paths and seaside sands of vacation ways—
draw near to us, Your children, here
  weary of the world and all its fear.
Lay loving hand on weary limb
  and touch the heart that seeks for You . . .

The Lord Who walked Himself on mountain ways
  and often saw the sea,
  and called to men
    to take the cross,
    and live life free, the same as He.

O Jesus Christ, we're a most respectable company
  here today, and the least of all we thought to see
  was You Yourself along our way.
    But You are here, aren't You? You're in this
    place. This chapel is Yours. And these people
    are Yours. And someone here, Lord, wants to
    know You today in the worst possible way.
  Maybe many, Lord, want You here, that You might
    come near and heal their fear,
    and dry their tear.

Don't let any of us get away, Lord, without facing You,
  and seeing You, and knowing that You love us and
  are calling us. Help us to know this is our hour—
  our time to decide.

Bless every family here, O Lord, we pray.
    Show little children how to walk Your way.
Bless our vacation time, protect on highway and in home
    all those who are Thine, and bring peace to our hearts
    and to the world, O Loving Lord.

Amen.

Lord Jesus Christ, our Saviour dear,
    right glad our heart that we can be here!
    In this forest glade neath towering pines
    and soft wind from the sea—to us a sign
    of the hand of God in the world around,
    and a Saviour's love by which we're bound.

O Lord, the Lord of every wistful seeking heart:
    We yearn within to do our part—
    to be good soldiers in the battle of life,
    to fight without fear in Thy Kingdom's strife.
Let this beautiful chapel, with its blood-red cross
    and the green on its floor, like the forest moss,
be a holy place on this summer morn
    where our world-weary spirits can be reborn!

We come to this city of ancient fame
    in a day far different, and not the same;
    remembering the days of her heroes brave,
    who risked life and fortune a country to save.
        John Paul Jones and his "Ranger" here,
        Governor Wentworth and his mansion near.
        Proud was this port on Piscataqua,
        this point of land where men first saw
            New Hampshire's beauties, its peaks and pines
            and the broad sand beaches of its white coastline.

O Lord, in Portsmouth of the past mid stately mansions that last and last,
    we people of today, so tamed, conformed,
    feel vague in our hearts we were higher born.
Born for more than just the little round—the inane, the innocuous,
    the trivial sound—
born for the brave, the bold deed and true,
    for living in courage with a great Lord like You!

Let not, O Lord Jesus, this hour go by,
    without each one hearing Your voice, and its cry.

In the City

And don't let us fear, Lord, to answer Your call,
    To promise to follow, and give You our all.
We need You, Lord Jesus, each one, in our lives. We've put You off too long.
    If there's a heart today, ready to walk in the way, win him this hour,
    O Lord, we pray. And in Your great love, Lord, make strong the weak,
    encourage the weary, heal those who are sick, bring joy to the dreary.
    And teach Lord, to each, the peace of this place,
        that the world so may come, seeking Your face.
        So may all men find peace by their hearts with ours banding
        in Him Whose great love passes all understanding.

                            Amen.

Eternal Father strong to save,
 O Son of God so good and brave,
 O moving Spirit o'er the restless wave: Look upon us.
 On this glorious summer day, jeweled with the morning sun,
 blowing in the leaves of cooling trees—
 with these windows open to a clean, pure, glistening world we come.
  And there is very little of glistening, or purity, or brightness
   about us!

So much of the golden glow of life is gone.
 So many things are taken for granted.
 So much we owe You that we haven't given.
 So many words we could have said.
 So many daring deeds we could have done.
 So many high roads we could have walked.
Look upon us, Lord. Forgive the past. Reconcile the enmity.
Encourage the good. Understand the human. And use us, Lord.
 Stop our wandering, wasting ways,
 and send us up into the mountains with Christ.
 Let the wind blow in our faces,
 and the sun shine in our valleys.
 Send us out along the high roads of the heart.
 Give us the old swing to our step—
 the swing that Jesus and His disciples must have had.
  And give us the brave song to sing—the
  song of the saints when they come marching in!

O God, away with every weakness of our lives! Every mean
 compromise, every false rationalization.
And make us brave to stand all the criticism,
 all the selfish clamor of these times between men,
 and make us unafraid in the face of it!
Let men find help in us.
Let them find us the allies of the poor,
 the friends of the disinherited,
 and the fellow soldiers of the underprivileged.

And have mercy on our cities, God, and guide them right.
As the storms of our time sweep even to our door and into our lives,
    keep us calm, and brave, and Christian
    even in the eye of the storm.
Bless the Church in its witness. Bless all people in peril.
Bless those suffering in sorrow. Overpower sickness in every life of pain.
    And so strengthen the company of Your people today,
    that by Your power we may overcome all things,
    and set Christ upon His throne at last,
        in the hearts of hundreds of the city's men
        who need Him.

    Amen.

Across a city silent from the din of busy days,
across smokestacks and high buildings thrusting toward the sky,
through teeming streets, and over the drumming trade of a whole city's life—
    You have come to stand amid the quiet walls of this holy house
    to keep the sacred tryst with us.
What glory fills our lives when You are here!
How silently the strange peace steals into our hearts,
and with what wonder we sense Your calm descending about our lives.

O Jesus, Lord, make this our Galilee!
    We remember the welcome of Your face when once You said:
    "Let the little children come to Me, for of such is the kingdom of
        heaven!"
We see that same look of kindness on Your face today,
    and hear that same word of welcome.
    And we see, too, the dust of our city upon Your clothes, and know
    that You have lived where we have lived,
    and that our shops and factories, our schools and homes are not
        strange to You.
    We see the company of Your friends whom You brought with you:
        a fisherman and a tax collector, a woman taken in adultery
        and a thief whose end was a cross, a traitor named Judas
        and the rich man Zaccheus.
O Christ, if such are Your band of friends,
    surely You will not exclude us!
    Surely we, too, can follow You!

Our sins, too, are such as these. We also have misused our wealth.
    We, too, have been selfish, clutching our pennies to ourselves
    and brushing by those whose needs were greater than our own.
    Adultery and secret lusting thoughts are among our sins.
    And even Judas' name we know, for more than once have we been
        traitor to the best we knew.

O Lord, we do repent! And gratefully we remember that
    "There shall be joy in heaven over one sinner that repenteth,
    more than over ninety and nine persons who need no repentance!"

And yet we pray You not to let our repentance become an aching,
continual brooding over sins that are past. Forgive us, Lord,
and help us accept Your forgiveness and then move on,
with our sins behind us and hope before us!
You said, "I am the light of the world. He that followeth Me shall not
walk in darkness, but shall have the light of life."
Be You our light. "Be Thou our vision, O Lord of our hearts!"
So we cast our cares upon You, O God. All the dark worries and
lonely anxieties of life we lay at Your feet. Heal us. Help us.
Gladden our hearts with the knowledge that You are our strength
and our salvation!
For a world of care we pray to You, O Lord.
For burdened hearts in every walk of life and in every land of Earth
we ask release and relief.
Open wide the gates of new life to them and to all our brother men,
and receive us into Your kingdom to live, and love, and labor
for Him Who is King and Lord forever.

Amen.

O God, Who from the Earth's first day has painted the blue of summer skies,
   Who Yourself has knelt on the good earth to plant grass upon our fields,
   and trees upon our mountains, and flowers along every country road:
   On this day of days, with beauty so surrounding us
   and joy so deep within us,
we gladly turn our hearts to You, with praise and thanks upon our lips!
This is Your day, Lord, and we are grateful to be alive in it.
   And ere our winter work begin, we would speak our thanks for
   summer days just past.

For every sight our eyes did see of ocean breakers on the coast,
   or northern peaks across the range, or sun-filled fields in valley ways—
we thank and praise You, Lord.
For every bird of the air or creeping thing we chanced to meet and watch,
   learning of animal ways and listening to wild songs and country sounds—
we thank and praise You, Lord.
For every day of rested body, and elm-shaded ease,
   and vacation indolence—we thank and praise You, Lord.
For shooting stars and northern lights, for lapping lakes and moonlit nights—
we praise You, too, O Lord.
For family times especially, Lord, we give You thanks.
   For companionship of trail or boat, for evening talk, and campfire
      light—
      we are most grateful, Lord.

And now, O God, Who also gives the city, and Who is Lord of all
   its power and its drive, we thank You for the work that waits us here,
   and for our call as Christian men to witness to this city.
We ask for relevance in our witness; we ask to be sent where people are,
   where the real lives of men are lived, where the great decisions of life
      are made—
   that the name of Christ may be heard in those places,
   until every knee shall bow
   and every tongue confess that Jesus Christ is Lord.

Eternal God, Whose justice holds in balance the destiny of men and nations,
   Whose power is love, and Whose strength is truth:

Look in compassion, we pray, upon Your world, stepping closer to
disaster every day.
Upon Berlin's people pour out Your courage and faith that they may
stand fast in You.
Upon our own President, be as his great rock in a weary land,
that he may lean upon You, and for his heart find strength.
For oppressed people everywhere, let freedom's light burn bright
within,
and lift their spirits high in hope.
And for us of this city and this church we ask our prayers for help.
For families whose door has been crossed by death this summer,
we ask Your comfort.
For those visited by any illness or infirmity, we ask Your healing.
For young people who leave for school or college, we ask Your hand
to shield,
Your light to guide.
In Christ's great Name.

Amen.

Prayers for Suburbanites

Lord Jesus, Saviour of the world,
     hope of every human heart,
     friend in every human need,
     the light of God in man's dark night,
     the hand of Heaven along Earth's rocky road,
     pure, and good, and Holy Spirit,
     the enemy of Earth's selfish, greedy, worldly spirit:
You are a great God, You Stable Child,
     You walker of the streets,
     You country carpenter
     Who goes everywhere, and all the world meets.

You're not too great and not too good
     to pray with the saint and hang around with the hood.
You're in the great companies, the executive suites,
     You're in Civil Rights marches, out in the streets.
Because You care—far more than we're aware.
     You care about us
     though we are so petty, and make so much fuss!
     You don't want us sick or afraid,
     You don't want us stuffy, self-righteous, or staid.
You want us set free, with our hearts all on fire.
     You want us praying, believing, climbing higher and higher.
     You want us to look up, and reach toward the sky.
     You don't want us asking always Why, O Lord, Why?

So Lord, if we're servants of Jesus, if we're to walk in His way,
        if His life is to be lived and His work done each day:
        Don't let us hang around, Lord. Get us out on the job.
        Let our hearts be converted, our lives find the faith.
        Help us pray all we can, and so win in the race—
        the race that is always won, if we run it with You.

So bless us, Lord. Bless the Church—poor old bumbling institution
     that she is! And make her alive, and singing, and saving, and serving,
     and victorious, here and everywhere.

            Amen.

                              For the Stuffy and the Proud

O God Who made the world as it is,
    and made us what we are;
    God of the winter sun shining across a snow-bound world;
    God of tall trees standing bare before the winter blue beyond;
    God of the frosty morning, like this one is,
        and yet God also of the world of men;
    God Who made us plain or beautiful,
    strong or weak, sure or uncertain,
    with our own faces, our own hands, our own hearts and feelings.
O God of our life, we thank You that we are alive:
    Alive in this beautiful world, alive on this magnificent day!
    And we praise and thank You that we are alive
    among this band of believers, and that we can call them our friends,
    and our brothers and sisters in Christ.

Lord, we've all been set in the midst of trying and troubled times.
    Wars and rumors of war sound across the airwaves of the world.
    And here at home tragic death stalks the highways,
    and a twisted sense of values distorts the decency of our own
        community.
    And yet, God, we know this is a great time to be alive!
        Never have ordinary men had such opportunity to affect the
        destiny of their time.
        Never have they had the chance to do so much to change the
        conscience of their community!

Don't let us lose our opportunity, O Christ,
    by being so puffed up with pride
    that we become false to our own truest instincts.
Don't let us be so swept away by the affluence we have created—
    by Cadillacs and Continentals, and
    button-down shirts and gray-flannel suits, and
    country clubs and cocktail parties, and
    Hondas and hell-raising, and
    Bermudas and frosted hair, and
    sports cars and ski weekends—
        that we forget who it is we really are.

O Lord Jesus, Who made us, each one, to be something absolutely unique in
         the world:
Let not the shallow show of social convention
     prostitute the person that we really are—
         that God the Creator made us, and
         that Christ the King called us to be.

Lord Jesus, we're here to be Your soldiers in this society, to be true to You
     and true to ourselves, and true to the great trust that is ours.
     For You we live, Lord, even in the midst of all this plenty.
     We submit it all to Your service.
         Please accept us.

         Amen.

O God, it's wonderful to be alive today! The smog hangs heavy in so many
> cities,
>> but we breathe the clean, clear air of north country.
>> We walk on green grass,
>> we look away to the West across Indian hills
>> and see the plains sweeping toward the setting sun!
>> We wake up in a village of warm and lovely homes.
>> We drive to our work in safe and beautiful cars.

And the world wants us, God! We have a place. We're somebody!
>> People look to us. They count on us. We play a part in life!

O God, glory be to You for life! And a thousand times glory be to You
> because we do not deserve it.
>> Oh, we've worked all right. Hard have we worked. Scraped, and saved,
>> and planned, and built, and started, and succeeded.

But we didn't do it, Lord. We know that. Healthy bodies we did not make
> ourselves. Keen minds and sharp wit and driving energy—we didn't
> manufacture these. They're a gift. And O God, what a gift!

O God, You've blessed us! What a privilege is ours. What privilege is
> our children's. Work, position, friends, home, school, even church!
> What a great thing to be part of a church that has loved Christ and
> tried to serve Him through twenty years, and has such an opportunity
> before it now!

O Lord Jesus, look upon us, a people of privilege, and see our heart.
>> Can't You use us, Lord, in some great way?
>> Can't You take these talents and this youth and spirit
>> and this money and make something of us?
>> Haven't You a mission for us?
>> A world in need for us to conquer for the Christ?

Take us, Lord. Take what we have, and build something great in this town,
> and in this city,
> and in our great nation
>> that will be to the glory, and the honor, and the very power
>> of Jesus Christ.

Amen.

For Seeing the Service of Suburbia

O God, from Whom the call goes out o'er land and sea, across wide plains,
 and even from house to house in sleeping Sabbath village,
 that men of faith are needed, and that now is the day,
 if ever our time is to be touched and our generation won,
 for a people like us to rise up and grasp the goal
 and claim the hour for Jesus!
Eagerly, Lord, and with ready hearts, this people waits the Word
 of where we are to serve, and what we are to do.

We are a motley crew, Lord—such a band of varied talent:
 city folk and country men not long since;
 society sophisticates and simple, solid souls;
 the good, and most of us so far from good;
 the brilliant, and most of us the slow and plodding kind.
 We wonder You could use us!
But we've heard the call, and we are ready to rise up and go.
Only go before us, do we ask. Christ before us, Christ behind us,
 Christ within us, Christ beside us.
   We are ready—show us the way!

And tell us what to say.
 O God, we don't know the answers to men's longing questions.
 We just stand there fumbling for that right word that only comes long
   after.
 Tell us the Truth for these times!
 Tell us what Thy Word in Scripture says to the seeking ones today.
 Tell us the Word the hungry are perishing to hear.
 And set us on fire with that Word,
  that, burning, we may be a brand defying the night
  and overcoming the dark until the great dawn comes.

Somewhere, O Lord, in this great company, there is someone—
 a young person perhaps, or maybe a father or mother—
 who is just looking for a place in which to throw his life,
 a cause in which to fling his faith.

To whom shall we go, Lord? To the prisoners, to the sick,
 to the poor, to the silent despairing lonely in the house next door?
 Or to some nursing station or teaching post in far off India?
 Capture our hearts today with the drama and the joy
 of giving up ourselves in order to serve!

Fan the flames of our faith, stir up the winds of the Spirit,
 and blow across the Church in America—
 And particularly the church in our village—
 until we move out in force to take the world!
  In the name of Him Who wins the victory—Jesus Christ.

            Amen.

Lord of all hopefulness, Lord of all joy,
Whose trust, ever child-like, no cares could destroy,
Be here at our waking, and give us, we pray,
Your bliss in our hearts, Lord, at the break of the day!*

Fill us with joy! Fill us with wonder, and awe, and unspeakable love
    as we kneel before Your Throne this day;
    as we kneel as brothers and sisters—a family of faith this day.
O, glorious and inexplicable are the ties that bind Your people, Lord!
    Wondrous is the power that brings us together here,
        that makes us love each other,
        that makes us *one people,*
            a church of the Living Christ indeed!

O Lord of the open road,
    Lord of the highways of the land and the highways of the heart,
    Lord of the northern pine and the starry night,
    Lord of the western sky and the morning sun,
    Lord of peace in the still woods,
    And most of all, Lord of the city and the busy lives of men. . . .

Lord of the business of life we come back to,
Lord of the Exchange and of the market,
Lord of the bargaining table and of the shop;
Lord of the hustle and the bustle,
        the tooling up of life,
        the shifting gears of commerce,
        the sweat of the brow,
        and the bread of the field,
        and the lights of home,
        and the hearth
        and the heart:

We come hence to You on this day,
    thankful that our greatest labors in life
    are our labors of love,
    our labors for the Lord,

*From the hymn "Lord of All Hopefulness," by Jan Struther.

our labors all the day long—
wherever there are men and wherever there are needs,
wherever a heart is broken, wherever a body is bruised,
wherever a spirit hangs heavy,
wherever a life could lose.

Thanks be to You, O God, that our task is Christ's task.
Thanks be to You, O God, that our standard is His cross,
                    that our banner is His flag,
                    and that our message is His song.
   Glory, glory, glory in this pilgrim band!
   Glory, glory, glory for a Christian land!

                    Amen.

O God, Who has made a winter world of gray November days,
    and turned our feelings from this waiting, windswept month
    to thoughts of skis and skates, and alpine slopes,
    and winter's exulting northern air:
We are reminded that it all is Yours, whatever the season brings.
    The Earth is the Lord's, and the fulness thereof;
    and we are the Lord's, whatever life's seasons may bring us.

And God, so many of us are in that troubled time of life
    when we are not so young any more,
    and our tummies are not so taut any more,
    and our hair is frosted not by the girl at the end of the line
    but by the God Who rules over time.
    And we are not carefree, but have become what we are going to be;
    and we look at our lives, and at the money we've made,
    and at our prosperous position so comfortable and staid,
    and we're not sure we want to settle for that.
        Is this all it's going to be, Lord?
        Responsibility, and respectability, and dependability?
        A life so solid, and sure, and sane, and safe
        that nothing will change, or ever chafe?

We don't know that we want that, Lord!
    We have it made, but we're not sure we want what we have made.
    Is there no adventure yet for us, O Lord: No daring, no drama,
    no chance to be a hero and escape the fate of a zero?
Haven't we been called to something greater,
    chosen for some mission by our Creator?
        We hope so, Lord. We hope for something more.
        We pray this day You will open the door,
            the door that will let Christ in
            and set us on fire, the world to win!
    Make it happen. Oh, make it happen, Lord!
    We pray that in our time, in our generation, all the great things
    of God will happen.

                                  For the Affluent

Show our generation, Lord—the "command generation"—
    how to count for Christ in a world of crisis.
      Use our power and our prayers in Georgia, in Johannesburg,
        in our city, and our suburb
          for the glory of our Lord, and of His Christ.
            For ever and ever.

              Amen.

O Master from the mountain-side,
   Make haste to heal these hearts of pain
Among these restless throngs abide
   O tread the city's streets again!*

O Jesus, Master, walk here upon our avenues and lanes,
   as once You walked in Galilee.
Come, Lord, where man's needs are, and do not stand aloof, afar!
We need You, Lord. The whole world needs You. Even so come, Lord Jesus!

O Master of men, Who cared with so great a heart for this world's needs;
   challenger of the money changers,
      healer of the broken and sick (even on Sabbath days),
      defier of social custom and religious tradition
         wherever human need and justice were at stake.
You Who came not to bring peace but a sword,
   Who came to set even fathers and sons against each other
   because Your principles challenge and divide.
You Disturber of the status quo,
   Who came so radically to change society
   that angry men could only see Christ on the Cross
   and out of their sight forever.

O Lord, don't let our faith be a cloak to keep us from the deed!
   Let us not stand on the side of the status quo,
               on the side of self-protection and prejudice
                  against any color or creed.
Help us to be guerillas in the greatest revolution of the ages—
   the revolution of the Church of Jesus Christ. . .Jesus and His men,
   Who came, as the first century testified, "to turn the world upside
      down!"

Help us, O Lord, to stand at the forefront of every movement
   to be brothers of the sons of men.

---

*From the hymn "Where Cross the Crowded Ways of Life."

For the Prejudiced

Put away from us our ancient prejudices and our false pride
about our Christian brothers who love the same Lord as we—
even though they worship Thee in different ways.
Help us to move out in glad greeting to meet and know our brethren
of the Church of Rome, that we may know their heart
and hold their hand and walk their way every time we can!

For the healing of the great hurt of history between Christian brothers,
we pray, O Lord, and ask grace, mercy, and peace
upon the people of our sister churches in our town,
and upon their pastors.
So be You our Guide and God, our all in all,
and let not one of us your servants falter or fall.

Amen.

O God our Lord, Who turns not away when any child of Yours
    calls out in prayer; Whose ear leans low to listen, and
    Whose hand, in strength and love, is always there:
We reach out today to take Your hand,
we cry out to You to hear our prayer,
    for we are Your children, and like children we often lose the way.

We are grateful, O great God, to be among Your friends.
    We are privileged to walk among the pilgrim people,
    to be numbered among the saints and charged to live true,
    and be brave, and follow the King.
We have been trusted with so much, O God.
    We have been called to a task so high. We wonder if it is not too high,
    and that we can never attain it.

And so we ask You only, Lord, that You will keep us in the field,
    that You will not let us flee the fight,
    but stay and stand through day or night.

So many voices tempt us back.
So many say this Christian cause is not our fight,
    that we should not be battling the forces of the dark, and light.
Whenever we set out to do some act for our Lord's sake,
    to take up some great cross and make it our banner and our cause,
    they say that we should pause.
    "You move too fast," they say. "It is not time."
    But if we wait for them, the hour You gave us will be lost!

Show us how, O Lord, to take the world for our parish.
Show us how to let our hearts brood over the whole world's need,
    and make it all our prayer, and our passion, and our care.
    And let us not be afraid to love the world, and lift it up,
    and die for it if we must.
    Teach us to care, as One cares for us, and died and lives for us.

Remember, too, our nation now,
    as again the yearning for public office stirs in men's hearts
    to lead the way, and bring in the new day.
    As we move toward the day of decision,
    make us wise and faithful in our choice.
Send the Church, we pray, into every corner of this country's way,
    to proclaim in marketplace and mansion-grace,
        in suburban park and city's dark,
    the news that Jesus cares, and that we, His people, also care.

                                        Amen.

Ah! Holy Jesus, how hast Thou offended?

Lord of the winsome heart, Lord of the laughing life,
Lord of the hills and the highways, of the cities and the slums,
    of the taverns and the towns;
Man of the world, Cosmopolitan of the cosmopolitans,
    Who dined with Pharisees and floozies,
    Who lived with reprobates and died with robbers,
    Who was ready to go wherever a man was in need,
    and Who saw all men's need, whether they saw it or not:
Is it because You make men so uncomfortable
That they turn on You and stab You with a cross?
Is that why they want You out of the way—
    because You search their hearts with Your eyes,
    because You ask their lives for the prize,
    because You expect what man denies?

Have we been offended, Lord? Have we thought You asked too much?
    Are we like that Church of long ago, neither hot nor cold
    but just lukewarm?
    Are we afraid to have You ask too much of us?

Lord Jesus Christ, You've seen all the masks we wear.
    You know what stuffed shirts we sometimes are,
    and how often we're on our dignity, and afraid to have anyone
    scratch the surface and discover we are men.
    And that we're scared, and that we need Someone
    very much to love us and forgive us, and start us out again
    with a pure heart and clean hands.

However we've come to church in the past, Lord,
    don't let us come dignified and defensive today.
    Don't let us have hearts of steel, and lives locked up in armor.
    Let us come to hear. Let us come seeking.
    Let us come humble enough to be born again!

For the Self-Sufficient

O thank You, Jesus,
　　for your promise that when we confess our sins
　　and believe in the Name of the Lord Jesus, we shall be saved!
Save us, Lord. Save us from ourselves.
　　　　　Save us from our hollow hearts,
　　　　　　and our empty lives,
　　　　　and make us Jesus' men today.

　　　　　　　Amen.

O God of Earth, of sky, Who has privileged us to live out
    where golden sun transforms the morning,
    and the stars stand still in deep darkness each night,
    and where a man can walk on green grass, and breathe clean air,
    and feel fresh winds, and look long toward far horizons:
We who live in a country place but are city men
    would pray today for the city that we love.

O God Whose heart of tender mercy broods over darkened tenement alleys
    and exhaust-filled crowded streets
    as surely as over open fields and suburban lawns and lakes:
    Bend low over our city, we pray, today.
Hear the vacant, secret cry of lonely longing, and make us hear it, too.
See the aimless, endless seeking of poor lost city souls.
    and make us see it, too.
Feel the pain of prejudice in human hearts, and make us feel it, too.

It is so easy, Lord, to forget about the broken, and sick, and poor
    of the city when you live in the luxury of the suburbs.
It is so easy not to feel the piercing thrust of prejudice,
    and the pangs of poverty,
    and the depths of human despair crying almost at your doorstep
    when you live in comfort, and have tasted the tang of success,
    and felt the glamor of good clothes, and known the pride of other men's
    respect and acceptance and friendship!

O Lord, the city is so different! And our conscience hurts us for the city.
    Show us how we can heal its hurts, and right its wrongs,
    and soften its hardness.
    Show us how our love can lift the lost,
    and how our compassion can conquer indifference,
    and how our faith can transform its future.

O faithful Father, forgive the self-centeredness of our lives.
    Forgive us for all we do for ourselves, and
    for so little we do for others.
    Forgive us for not caring enough to go into
    all the world to preach the Gospel.

Help us this day, we pray, to see the Christ Who died for the world,
    Who came not to bring the righteous but sinners to repentance,
    Who came to love the lost, and save the sinful,
        and bring all men home to You.
And make us love with His love until we too are burdened—
    to preach the Gospel to the poor, to heal the brokenhearted,
    to preach deliverance to the captives, and recovering of
        sight to the blind,
    and to set all men at liberty until the kingdom comes.

Amen.

Lord, out in the world we've been, this week.
>   In the marketplace, on the exchange, at business breakfasts,
>   on the road, in the air, around town, almost everywhere—
>>   in Boston, New York, Richmond, Las Vegas, San Francisco,
>>   Switzerland, Milan, Hawaii.
But we're home now. Thank You for bringing us safely home.
>   We're home with our families, we're home with our church.

We love Your Church, O Lord. Not the building, though we're glad for it,
>   but the people. The people of God. The beloved community.
>   The concerned community. The forgiving community—
this whole crowd of people with their strange mixture
>>   of needs and deeds, of hurts and hopes,
>>   of failures and success.
They're Your people, Jesus, and they're ours. We thank You for them.

We thank You that they're praying now,
>>   that they believe prayer makes a difference,
>>   that they care enough to pray,
>>   that they know men will be healed
>>   and lives will be changed
>>   and the world will be won through prayer.

God, hear our prayer for Viet Nam. For soldiers dying there,
>   for civilians being riddled to death there,
>   for a land being torn apart there.
Hold that land in the hollow of Your hand!

And for the sick we pray.
>   Lord love them, and heal them, and hold them close to You.

And God, hear our prayer for the Church.
>   Come, Holy Spirit, Heavenly Dove,
>   and pour out on us Your power and Your love.
>   Help us to come alive! Fill us. Send us before You.
>>   We pray it for Your love's sake.

Amen.

For the Far-Flung Life We Live

Prayers for the Early Morning

O Lord of the dawning hours, when the world is still, and across the hill
    comes day's first light, and brings an end to the dark of night . . .
we wait in wonder as each day comes.
      This day, too, was a miracle, Lord, with pale light behind the trees,
      and then the dawn that always sees the movements of the early
            morning—
          from householders taking in the morning papers
          to milkmen on their rounds,
          to little dogs let out for the day's first run,
          to passing cars moving ghostlike through gray dawn
              on some special mission to us unknown.

It's a wondrous, waking world, O God, and it's Yours!
    This world is Your kingdom,
    and that's why it is crowned with glory in every dawn;
    that's why men move with a kind of stealth
        and unspoken reverence
        into a world and a day
        that they know is not their own.
And Lord, this day, especially, seems crowned with glory
    for the coming of the King, Your Son, Yourself,
    as Man among us men,
    as Child among all Earth's children,
    as Light to people who walk in darkness,
    as Prince of Peace over a world at war, and
    as Lord of Hope to men lost in sin.

O God, we wonder about so many dawns that came up over Jesus' life.
    Did He wake early and walk out in the dark to meet the day?
    Was He a dawn-man, a lad Who busied Himself about the village
        in the first waking hours before the sun was fully up?

We thank You that as a man He made those hours His hours of prayer.
We thank You that on the hills, or by the sea,
    He was up with the birds' first sound,
    that He could be counted on to be around.

For a World Waking Up

And He's around now, Lord.
    The Saviour Who is coming is already here,
    The King Who comes already reigns.
    And this day,
        and this hour,
            and this beautiful place are full
of all the glory of God!
    Glory, glory, glory in the land we love, today!

                            Amen.

O Great God, Who must once have stood out upon the primeval loneliness,
    and with the hands of a great artist flung the stars against the night,
    and made the East to glow with the fingers of the dawn,
    and shaped with master touch the green grass
    and the everlasting hills and the tall trees of five continents,
    and Who must—with a Father's loving heart—
        have made a man to walk with You,
        and given him a heart to hear Your voice,
        and then to have become his God and his Good Friend
        and showered upon him all the gifts that
        men through ages since have shared:
We marvel at what You have done for us!
    What a world!
    What a day in which to be alive!
    What a beautiful autumn season for our souls!

O God, the whole world is Yours.
    The cattle on a thousand hills are Yours.
    The sunrise in the morning is Yours,
    and the hovering of the harvest moon in evening is Yours.
    The great rivers are Yours.
    The lights of every city are Yours—
        its people and its problems, its offices and its factories.

And all this world has been given to us!
    This is our world, God, and we hardly know how to take that.
    Tell us what to do with it! Show us how to be grateful.
    Don't let us be those who take it all for granted.
    Don't let us be a people on the Divine dole—
    just taking, taking, taking, and never giving back.

We don't have anything, God, that we got alone.
We didn't climb high on the ladder of life because we are so smart.
We don't have lovely homes and beautiful children and impressive
    futures because we're brighter than all the rest.
Your hand has been there all the time,
    and that hand has led our lives, and given us the friends we love,
    and the wealth we enjoy, and the Church we serve.

For Musing on the Mystery of Day's First Dawn

And so, we give ourselves to You!
>If some have a voice, let them sing out praise to Thee.
>If some have hearts, let them bear the load to set the burdened free.
>If some have hands, let them hold the sick and weary tenderly.

With those hands and hearts
>we give back our lives to You, and
>promise to live beneath the cross, without a fear, in this life and
>eternally.

>Amen.

O God Most High,
    Who out of nothingness fashioned a world in beauty,
    Who out of the mists of time
        and the darkness of eternity
        made the Earth's first dawn to shine across a whole new creation;
You Who turned the shadow of night into morning
    and let even the darkness be flooded with the light of the moon:
We, Your privileged children,
    whose joy it is to walk through summer meadows of growing grass,
        to see glinting sun upon the distant hills,
        and the rippling of moonlight on lakes and streams
        when the shadows lengthen and the evening comes—
we turn our hearts to You
on this day of beauty,
to pour out to You our song of praise and thanks!

For Life, and all it means to us,
for friends who love us,
for work that challenges us,
for homes that shelter us,
for life's tiny triumphs that encourage us,
for others' bravery that inspires us,
and for the pilgrim band,
our brothers of the common way—
    the Church of Christ:
        we thank You, Lord!
For every comrade of the Christ
    who sees it as his duty and desire
    to bow his head with us in prayer this day,
    we give our most especial thanks.

Fashion us, we beg You, into a company of the concerned.
    Heap upon our hearts the cares of all the world,
    that we may bear them in joy to You in prayer.

Grant to us a world concern,
   a great gratitude,
   and make our song of praise be
      for all men . . .
        all lands . . .
        all life . . .
           everywhere!

        Amen. Amen.

O God of the good Earth, Who promised that

while the Earth remaineth,
seed time and harvest,
cold and heat, summer and winter,
and day and night, shall not cease

among Your children;
and Who, by a rainbow in the sky,
has made covenant with man
that You will be his God,
and he, and his children, will be Your people:
We claim You for our own, O Lord.
We claim our place among the children of Your love.
And on this day of thankfulness we render praise for all it means to us.
For waking up to find Your glory streaming o'er the Earth,
for summer sun, and autumn gold,
for the harvest of the land by which we live.
For little children who fill our years with laughter and with fun,
for bodies strong by which we think, and walk, and run.
For people who love us, and understand when we are unlovable, and
forgive.
For a beautiful city of lakes in this land of the north
where we can grow up, and work, and live.
For someone who values what we do, and pays us to do it well.
For ambitions, plans, and hopeful dreams on which our hearts can
dwell.
For a country free, and brave, and strong that stands for right
and not for wrong.
For a church with greatness in her heart and with people eager,
and willing, to do their part.
And for Jesus, Who goes before,
our light and life, more and more—
for these we thank You, and ask this humble people's prayer.

Amen.

For God's Goodness in the Morning

O God of the autumn wonder,
 Who makes the valleys blaze with beauty
  and turns the lazy summer into the long and golden afternoons of fall;
 Who fills the far hills with game,
 Who turns the pheasant on the wing,
  and makes walking in woods among fallen leaves a wonderful thing:

We thank You for these days!
We thank You for crisp air, and blue sky, and
 for something within the heart of man
 that loves Your outdoor world.

Bless those who tramp the woods and fields today, O God.
 Protect them from stray shot or unmeaning injury.
 Grant them fair weather
   and good companions,
   and let clear air clean out their souls,
   and the wonder of the world give wings to their feet,
   and splendor of the skies start a song in their hearts!
 And bring them home refreshed,
  and restored,
  and ready to bear with light hearts
  the burdens of the world.

Look in love, we pray, upon all men everywhere,
 but especially the men of this company, our comrades.
 Remind us all that our Saviour was a man
  —a man's man among men—
 Whose hands were skilled at the carpenter's bench,
 Whose heart loved laughter,
 Whose voice sang songs, and
 Whose life was lived with other men.

Let Your Church, O Lord, be a place for men,
 for there's a man's work to be done
  and a man's world to be won!
   For Jesus and His Kingdom.

    Amen.

For the Aura of Autumn

God, Whose glory fills the sky,
 and Whose great hand sweeps across the landscape
 to make the magic of the morning:
 We gather in this house of Puritan Pilgrim worship,
  glad for the open windows that let in the morning glory,
  glad for the white and simple beauty of this meetinghouse
  that makes a place for the beauty of the earth,
     the sparkle of the sun,
     the trembling of the trees,
     and the soaring of the sky!
Glory, God, to You! Glory, God, to You, O Lord most high!

And glory, God, to You, O Lord,
 for the gathering of Your people in this place we love,
 in this hour for which we've waited all the week!
We thank You that these are our friends.
We thank You that there is love in this house
 among the brethren, the Master's men.

We remember that we are under orders today, O Lord;
   that we have been called up to serve our Saviour,
   to go out and fight for Him, and live for Him,
   and love for Him, and heal the world for Him,
   and perhaps to die for Him.
Help us to know we have been called, that living for You is our calling.
Help us be the equal of the world, more than its match in loyalty and love,
 in holiness and helpfulness, in perseverance and in power!

We look up from this place where our hearts so often have found their peace
 and look out across this golden day to those places of peril where
 there is no peace.
 And our hearts would hold those people in love and hope:
 The people of Eastern Europe—
 Spirits in prison behind a curtain of iron;
 For poor little Laos and Viet Nam, plundered with corruption and
  riddled with war;
 For everywhere else that the barbed wire of human hate keeps men
   divided from each other.

For Wordly Wonder Through a Window

Look upon us, Lord—all our world of troubled, lonely, fear-filled people—
and heal us. Heal us here, too, of every jealousy, every prejudice,
every anger, and every failure in faith.
And so bless us in our praying and our preaching,
in our singing and our listening
in our loving and our laughing,
that we may leave this house today as a people called to glory,
and so a people glad and ready and anchor-sure within.

Amen.

All Merciful One,
Who stood as silent Sentry keeping watch at the gates of life
through the hours of uncertain darkness while we slept;
Who willed our lives to last another day,
     crowned in glory, on our way:

Thanks to You for all the promise of fresh and new beginnings,
which the morning splendor streams into our darkened souls.
Thanks to You for dawning's brilliance sparkling through
the branches of our trees and across the dew of grass,
telling our hearts a new day has come,
that God gave it, and it's ours to use as one more span
of lighted hours in which to serve and glorify
our God and King, the Lord of Earth and sky!

O Gracious Lord and Master,
Who also gloried in early sun rising o'er the misty shores
and untroubled waters of Gennesareth:
May our day today begin as Yours so often did—
in the quiet majesty of uplifted prayer.

Lord Jesus, Whose every hour was lived for Your Father in Heaven:
We, too, would live this day for You.
Help us draw strength from this hour apart,
that into the dust and turmoil of a humdrum world we may go
as You always went . . . full of the power, and poise, and serenity within
that God alone can give.

Make us like You, O Lord, that we may leave undone
all the petty little deeds that waste our time
and dissipate our energies; and do instead
works worthy of Christians who may never have another day to live.

Show us what is most important; take us where we are
most needed. Where there are sick or burdened souls
whom we could help, steer our feet into the pathway of their lives,
that we may walk with them.

For a New Day's Chance to Begin Again

Where there are lost souls who have no one to pray for them,
bow down our heads and bend our knees to plead for them
with that same love with which You are ever forgiving and winning us.

Lay the burdens of the world upon our hearts, O Lord.
And forget us not when shadows fall and evening comes, and our day at last
        is done,
    and Your victory in us is won.

Amen.

Almighty God, Who meets us in the dawning hours
     of the first day of the week
     while the morning is yet fresh upon the Earth,
     and the sun leans low across the land,
     and the birds sing,
     and the winter makes promises of the spring;
     and for a momentary halt our lives are hushed;
     and from the clanging traffic of our times,
     and from the rushing roar of always more and more,
          we turn aside with something eager in our hearts,
          something hopeful in our steps
          to this colonial meetinghouse
          where men were meant to meet their God,
          where the weary were to come for rest,
          the sinful to seek salvation,
          the suffering to find some solace,
          and the weak to be made strong.

O God, Who has so often met us here at break of day,
     when we come to learn of our Lord to pray,
     and with Him to follow in the way—
          come to us, O God, with a Word to say!
Speak to us of Jesus,
     and the disciples He called His men.
     Speak to us of the cross, and of how we can bear it up again.
     Speak to us of love, and how it heals where men are hurt.
     And speak to us of trusting God, to be our Lord and lead us on to life.

Out of the news of an erupting world,
     we ask for a message that speaks to the real world of real men.
     Speak a word of help to our President, that he
     may hear and know that he stands strong surrounded for his task.
Forget not the men of Congress in their days of decision.
     And be pleased to stand near those little people who think
     they do not shake this world's events.
     Shake the hearts and hopes of all of us who love them.

For a Quiet Moment in the Clanging Traffic of Our Time

And Lord, let the sun in the sky and the balm of the breeze
    be the promise of hope for every heart that sees its rays and rises
        with burdens gone and heart at peace.
    Through Christ's strong friendship, which we all need
    if we're to do today His demanding deed.

Amen. Amen.

Prayers at Sunset-Time

Lord Jesus, as still the night comes down
 and the blazing heat of day goes away,
 I stand on the sand
 and watch the last light before night
 flood the far hills,
 and with golden glory fill
 the cup of the sunset lake
 with more beauty than my heart can take.

And I cry: O God, You're great.

  O Jesus, Lord, You hold it all in Your hand,
   this beautiful land,
  and my soul is seeing
   what the fresh-washed world
  must have seen when the Earth
   itself was first unfurled!

O streaming sun, slanting low from the west
 across these hills I love
 and this lake my home,
  my cup overflows with light, and love!

For God is in this hour.

 This healing, evening light shows me His power.
 And the hand of God touches me
  and sets me free
  from civilizing sickness and city sin,
  and gives me grace and hope
  again, to begin.

Thoughts of God in the Gloaming

O healing hills of home!
O lake I love!
O precious hour alone,
with the Lord from above!
    Beauty!

        Joy!

            Peace!

                And thanks!

        Amen.

O God, my God, Whose ear bends low through every century
to hear Your people's cry;
 Who heard the plea of Moses in the pharoah's land,
 Who heard Elijah's cry before the cave,
 and the breaking heart of Hosea praying for his people,
 and Christ's own call from the cross:
Hear now Your people's prayer today, as with one full heart
we raise our cry to You.

You Who so graciously have guarded the ways Your people walked through
 centuries past,
You walk with us as surely as You walked with them!
You are our God as truly as You were ever theirs!
And on this night at sunset-time, as over the hills the darkness comes,
we grateful people at the hour of prayer turn aside in trust
 to ask and wait Your blessing.
O morning joy, and peace in evening's benediction,
strength in our days of testing, comfort in the nights of sorrow,
guide on every darkened highway of the heart,
and our great hope and healing beyond all the hurts of life:
 With evening joy and calm we bless Your Name.
 O glory, glory, Lord!

O Jesus, Saviour, as at eventide in Capernaum town the sick and troubled
came close to Peter's house to find Your touch upon their lives,
we, too, bring near our friends dear of church and town,
 that they may hear, and by Your hands be healed.
In the silence of this holy hour we speak the names of those who need You—
 for all our friends who at this hour are sick,
 for other friends who are in great trouble,
 for those feeling old and useless now,
 and for the young who do not know it is later than they think. . . .
 For little children and their parents,
 and for all who've had a blessing in their lives today
 and share a truth and know a joy—we voice our prayers.

And, evening Christ, Who comes to lakeside and to mountain rest,
to every quiet place where human hearts do seek their God,
hold in Your hands the world tonight.
>   And may it, next to Your heart, have hope and help
>   for all its needs tonight—because You are God,
>   and because in death and life, and soaring hope, You care!

Amen.

God of all that is: Of circling planets in a universe of stars,
 of blooming daffodils in spring,
 of little children growing up—O God of every miracle of life!

God of all that is: of rising sun and evening dusk,
 of fireflies before the sun comes out,
 of cragged mountains 'gainst a glorious sky—O God of every
  miracle of beauty.

O God, again, of all that is: Of honest hearts that know the right,
 of lives that dare, for what they cannot see, to sacrifice,
 of human souls fashioned for a future in eternity—
  O God of every miracle of truth.
O God of all that is, we praise Your Name!
You We praise for life, for beauty, and for truth!

O God, for all You've done for us, hear now our thanks:
 for this day, God, for its beauty beyond the gray of clouds,
 for its promises of new growth, new friendship, and new chances
  to live for You!
 And God, for our homes—for the fathers and mothers,
 and grandparents and aunts, and brothers and sons
 who sometimes are taken for granted, yet mean so much to us—
we thank You, yes, thank You!
For the work we've had this week, for its disciplines and delights,
 for its honest satisfaction, and for the glorious chance it gives to us
 to do for others—we thank You, yes, we do!

And Lord, for the privilege of these open skies,
 this day, this night, this life, this hope, this faith—we thank You!

O Lord, Who is never satisfied with us the way we are,
 Who, with such vast patience and love
 is ever changing us, and teaching, and showing us new truth, new
  duties:

Show us how to live the Christian life.
Show us how to walk with Christ,
    to live His life, and love His friends.
Show us our weakness and our failures,
    our hatreds and our unkindness,
    and help us love You better!
And thank You for it all—
    Good Lord, Great God, and our Saviour!

                    Amen.

O God, Who filled the night with stars
    and the day with dawn,
Who made the darkness to be not a cover
    for the devious deeds of evil men
but a time of wonder for the mysterious deeds
    of a mighty God:
Our hearts praise You for the midnight marvel of these
    nights of mystery.
We praise You for the listening stillness of these special nights,
we praise You for the clear cold that tells us winter's here,
we praise You for the stars in the night sky that remind us
    of another star,
    and another night,
    long ago.

Help us, O God, to move out as seekers for a star.
    Let the hunger of the soul, and the yearning of the heart,
        and the lifting up of hope
        be our spirit in these seeking days.
    Let us be forever looking up,
        and scanning the skies,
        and gazing at the far horizon
        for signs of truth and knowledge.
    Make us seeking men, traveling men,
        pioneers of the Spirit,
        adventurers on the highway of the heart,
        not afraid to live on the frontiers of faith,
        daring the unknown,
        hungering for the highest—
        looking for that light that shone
        once on a great night,
        and can shine again in every heart
        that waits and watches honestly and eagerly.

Come to our hearts, Lord Jesus. There is room in our hearts for You!
Come to our lives, O Saviour, for only in You do we live!
Come even here, O mighty Spirit, and fill us with Your love,
    and with Your power, and with Your joy.

Prayers on a Still, Dark Night

O little Lord, for Whom so many waited,
    help us to wait with patience and eagerness and expectation
    for the stars to sing to us,
    and the night be still for us,
    So we may hear Your coming
    and live life new by Your loving!

                    Amen.

O loving Lord,
    Who on a still dark night lit only by the stars,
    gave in silence before shepherds' eyes and mighty kings,
        a tiny Saviour to the world:
    We who've found our darkness turned to light by Him,
            our lostness turned to life by Him,
               and our loneliness turned to laughter by Him,
      give thanks and praise for sending Jesus!

For His shepherd's crook,
    and His kingly crown,
    and the cross of triumph that was His throne,
we thank You, Lord.

We thank You
    that with His shepherd's heart
    He takes the crook and leads us on;
    that with His crown of thorns
    He shows His love for us in suffering pain;
    that on the cross that is His throne
    He reigns, our Lord and liege forever.

O giver of such a perfect gift as Christ,
    let us be good men, too.
    Let the crook and the crown be signs of our love, too:
        the love with which we reach out to other's need,
        the sacrifice and service with which we do our deed
           beneath the banners of the cross, for Christ.

We would be a conquering host for the Christ, O Lord.
    We would be unafraid to dare new deeds for Him,
            unafraid to walk life's ways unknown
         if He is by our side,
         unafraid to be great men
         if He should call us to be great.

Thanks for the heart's great harvest
    waiting to be gathered in, O God!
And thanks for the comrades of the cross
    who go out with us to reap, today.
Thanks for the vision—the sign in the night—
    you've let us see!

    Amen. Amen.

O healing God, Who gives grace to men to go apart
    from the turbulence of their times into high places
    to reflect on who they are, and how they've lived,
        and where they're going:
Grateful are we for those numbered times the heart remembers
    when we've been privileged to hike into the heart's high hills,
    and see the vision and discover God again,
    and understand ourselves again, and find life full of hope again,
    and happiness again, and high purpose again.

Whatever that time has been for us, Lord—
    whether long in the past, or in the days of this week—
    we thank You, Lord,
and ask that we be true to the vision that it brought and to the life it
        promised.
Help us here to ask the great questions, Lord:
    why we exist, the subtleties of sin, and the possibilities of goodness.
Help us remember the man named Jesus,
    Who thought it not demeaning to strive for goodness, to pray for purity,
        to be always gentle even though strong,
        to be always kind even though courageous,
        to be always compassionate even though truthful.

Let cursing die upon our lips, O Lord.
    Let sarcasm, and derision, and the bullying spirit perish from our hearts.
    And let every habit of life that weakens the body,
        or erodes the spirit, or dulls the mind
        lose favor forever in our eyes!

O God, as in Adam so much of good in us has died,
    so in Christ may it come to life.
Forgive us our failures and sins of the past, we pray,
    and make us a new heart, and renew a right spirit within us.
Make us glad for life, and for the Lord Who taught us how to live it!
And let our ears hear again the sound of distant singing,
    let our eyes see again the ancient visions.
    And may we do the deeds and serve the King as He deserves.

For Time to Go Apart and Rest Awhile

Make us see, here, in this quiet place apart, the eternal truths;
   and know that we can be brave men in truth's cause,
      soldiers of the Christ on the battlefields of life.
   Inspire the young, stir up the fires in the old,
   and give us courage to carry the cross again,
      until tyranny, fear, prejudice, injustice, and wrong
         are doomed and done, and Christ is all in all.

O thank You for this peace, and for this power!

Amen.

Prayers When Your Heart Is Happy

O Jesus, Lord of Joy,
>   Who walked like sunshine through the world,
>   shining the light of love upon hundreds and thousands
>> of insignificant, nameless lives
>> until each one caught a ray of splendor
>> and lit a special light of glory in his dark corner!

O laughing, loving Jesus,
>   Who never walked the world with a long sad face,
>   but carried a smile into the homes and hearts of men!

O Christ with the face to the sun: tall, strong, tanned man among men—
>   happy man, singing man, man with hands of a carpenter
>   and heart of the Christ.

Thanks for Your joy!
Thanks for Your swinging step, and Your mountain life;
>   for Your heart heading always higher,
>>   Your Spirit ranging always on ahead!

Praise to the Hero of our hearts!
Honor and majesty to Your Name, Lord of our lives!

O Heart of God in the life of a Man,
>   be our Friend and our Saviour as we walk the way together.
>   Help us see the light beyond the cross,
>   just as we see the darkness of a day on Calvary's hill,
>   and Your body on that tree, as we walk toward that holy city afraid—
>   knowing very well it will be, for You, the city of hell and not holiness!
>   Make us penitent. Teach us humility. Hear our confession.

But let us at no time forget the paradox of our faith;
>   That our faith is a song; that our fight is a victory;
>   and that our cross is empty, because our Christ lives!

O conquering Christ, Victor over all the principalities and powers of life;
>   Saviour of men, Redeemer of the lost,
>   Lord of Heaven and earth: Win the victory in us!
>   Strike dead the temptations in our hearts!
>   Slay the sly doubts that assail us, the awful uncertainties that assault us!

Amazing Grace

O Lord, there is no conqueror of Christ—not even death.
    We claim Your victory over the dark, irrational forces
    that have produced war in the world.
        We turn them over to You for Your victory.
    Destroy every hatred of the heart; every shred of self-righteousness;
        every nerve of greed, and jealousy, and selfishness that produces
            war.
    And guide aright those who would be men of peace.

Thank You for hearing our prayer, and walk with us in the way,
    that our witness always may be for good over evil, joy over sorrow,
    peace over pain, and life over death—especially the death of the cross.
Glory be to You! Hallelujah!

    Amen.

O God, our God, You have the whole world in Your hands!
>You have the little bitty babies in Your hand,
>You have my brothers and my sisters in Your hand,
>You have everybody here in Your hand:
>>You've got the whole world in Your hands!

And not a sparrow falls in all that world, but You know he's fallen.
>Not a hair is harmed, but You know it's harmed.
And not one of us stumbles and falls, but You're always there,
>with Your outstretched hand holding ours in Yours
>and pulling us along—with a song!

Grateful we are that we count with You.
Amazed we are that mid all the galaxies of the universe
>Your heart holds ours in love.
Glad we are that Your Spirit walks with our spirit, and is our song and shield,
>our armor and defense, our safety, and our sword.

Nothing can we hide from You, Lord.
As the Lord's army, each day we stand inspection.
And so often our feet are not shod with the preparation of the Gospel of
>>peace,
and our sword is not the two-edged sword of the Spirit,
and our shield so often has no cross upon it.

O Lord, we know we often have not stood our ground as Christ stood His.
>>We know we have shunned to face the high priests of life,
>and we know we have held back from life's crosses
>so that no man could nail us there.
In such a web of compromise we all have caught ourselves, O God.

Set us free, O God! Show us the way out of the maze.
Lead us out along the high road of the conscience,
>and set us free from ourselves!
Walk with us until we know we do not walk alone;
hold tight our hand until our strength comes as the strength of ten!

Lift high our sights until all we see is the horizon and the hope of life,
and the sun and the sky, and the promise of new life beyond, that
is the hope of every Christian heart.

O God, Who holds us all and would bring us closer as a band of brothers,
bless our coming together now;
make love to live among us,
and patient understanding fill our hearts—always.

Amen.

O God of this good morning:
With the warm spring upon the land, and
with glorious sun slanting across our dawn-filled day,
    we sing to You a song of praise.
    Glory, glory to Your Name, O Lord.
Because we are alive! Because we are not sick, or maimed, or broken;
because we have the privilege of carrying on for a great Christ;
because we have been spared spring floods along our own streets,
    nor live behind dikes like thousands of our friends;
because we are free to hold up our heads and be men among men—
    to enter any restaurant, to travel any bus, and to vote in any election!

O Jesus Christ, Who came not to bring the righteous but sinners to
    repentance;
O Jesus, Saviour, Who came because God so loved the world:
    Make us passionate crusaders for the cross of Christ our Lord!
    Let not the sword sleep in our hand till we have built Jerusalem
        in this, our green and pleasant land!

O Lord, help us to see that in Your sight
    We are not free because we are good.
    We are not safe because we are shrewd.
These are Your gifts to all men. Help us to
        hear the call
    to fight and work till they are shared by all.

O Christ of the high roads of the world,
    Christ Who still swings out into the unknown morning,
        with every son of God who goes forth to work;
    Christ Who strengthens our weak knees,
        and makes sure our faltering feet, and lifts up our downcast hearts,
        and makes our spirits sing!
    Christ of the prophets and apostles of old, make us apostles!
In these resurrection days, these latter days of Your coming again,
    with our hearts still burning within us at Your sight upon our Emmaus
        roads,
    make us people of the Book, men with a message,

Christians who deeply care about Your Word to the world,
Your message to men!
Make us messengers of Good News in this town, and in our city,
and in every city—east or west, at home or abroad—
where commerce or concern may take us.

And let that Good News be for the healing of the nations
and for the healing of every broken heart, until it sings like ours today!

Amen.

O God of this wonderful day!
God of the warm earth, and the melting snow, and the blue sky;
God of springtime winging of the birds back north,
God of every sound and song of the Earth on this day of beauty and promise:
    Praise to You!
    Thanks to You for Your glory in field and flower,
    and the promise of many and many a sun-filled hour!

We thank You for such a host of good things in our lives.
We thank You that we are alive, that we are well,
        that we are free, that no despair dogs us
        and no darkness overcomes us,
        that no tragedy can turn our song to silence.
We thank You that we can sing a song of the saints of God
        and know that Your blessing is round about our lives, too—
        in glorious, fulfilling ways.

We thank You for the Church of Christ.
We thank You for the ministry of power around the world
        that it tells among men everywhere, that Jesus Christ is Lord!

We thank You for our own particular Church of Christ.
        This Church of free men
        bound by covenant promise,
        walking a pilgrim way together,
        trying as a people to be men of Christ, soldiers of the Lord.

We thank You for Your hand in human history,
        for Your care about all our lives and our least concerns.
And Lord, make us brave, and dedicated, and sincere enough
        to so let Christ into our lives
        that He will become a living, vital reality,
        that we can say: One thing I know!
            That I am Christ's, and He is mine!
        Let the victory be always ours, Lord, in Jesus' Name.

                                        Amen.

Showers of Blessing

God, we have received so much from Thee!
 Whenever we open our minds to look about us
 at the moments that fill our days,
 such myriad blessings do we see!
How many times we've found ourselves with some angel unawares
 in the person of a friend of many years who understands our need,
 or of a neighbor whose smile floods with light
  the darkness of some difficult day,
 or the tiny clutching of a baby's hands, holding tight.
O Lord, what kindness sometimes moves the hearts of men,
 and what treasured pearls of great price are the quiet words,
 the generous deeds, and the loving looks
 that make our lives exciting, and good, and worth the living!

These are all Your blessings, Lord.
 No good deed is done but by Your love inspiring some human heart.
 All thanks and praise to You, most gracious God,
  for these good things of life.

O giver of every good and perfect gift,
 we are well aware how easily we take
 and yet how grudgingly we often give.
We do not come boldly to this place.
We do not come with pretensions of virtue,
 or with great expectations of reward.
We come in fear and trembling, for we know that this is holy ground.
We come to be forgiven; we come to be healed and blessed;
we come praying that the gates of new life will open at our knock
 and swing wide to receive us and fulfill our need.

O Jesus, Lord, we would not cease our prayer with asking only for ourselves.
 We bow before You to plead for our friends in Christ and for all the
  world.
 Be near those, O Lord, Who kneel beside us now.

And those, too, who are not here: for the old who cannot come,
for the young who can but see no point in coming,
for the sorrowing who cannot bear to come,
and for the sick whose lonely battles for life take all their
    strength and faith.

And finally, Lord, for all the world we pray:
    for the nations and for men, for presidents and for kings;
    and for Christ's Church out there, everywhere men have need.
Glory be to You, Lord, that You are there, and that You care!

Amen.

O God, Who turns the Earth to springtime and the heart to hope,
    Who makes the day grow long and the sun set late,
        and brings the birds back north, and makes Earth sing the songs of
            life:
Glad are we for the season's turning,
and for the hope of these days of the human heart!

There is a wonder to this season, Lord:
    A special sense that this is the time of the seeking heart
    and the waking life, the time of new birth—even the birth of men's
        souls.
It is the season when out of every human sorrow, and the burden of secret
        sin,
    and every cloud of darkness, there comes up a dawn.
    The morning comes on a distant mountain,
    a trumpet sounds on a far-off rampart, and glory comes,
    and a Prince of Peace rules the world, and reborn hearts know that
    He shall reign for ever and ever! Hallelujah!

O conquering Christ, Who comes to walk the ways of men
    especially in a season such as this:
    A hundred hungry hearts wait in this place for You.
    We wait to be touched by You.
    We wait with hoping hearts for the hand of the Christ
        to show itself in our human lives, to show us that He lives.
        To show it's not a dream, and not a delusion,
    but the most decisive drama of human history,
    the Divine drama of a holy God Who loves us with such a love
        that dying for us was not too great to do.

O Risen, Loving Lord: We would see Jesus.
                We would see the face of the Master.
                We would hear the call of the Christ.
                We would feel the winds of the Spirit.
    Sweep us along with You, Lord! Give us the vision!
    Set in our hearts the dreams, and make us today Your own!

When the Earth Turns the Heart

O hand of God, grateful are we for Your sustaining strength for our men in
      space
      as they ride down from danger to the Earth again.
      Grateful are we for Your reconciling power at work in every capital of
         the world, to bring the healing of the nations and the reconciling
            of men.
      Grateful are we for Your Church in the world—
         especially the Church in China, in Germany, in Russia,
         the Church in the cities of America and in our village.
Make us all to be Your shining witnesses to the power of the Holy Spirit today,
      and all through the season.
Help us to see Jesus in the early morning, "Still as of old He calleth, follow
      Me."
      Let us arise, all meaner service scorning.
      Lord, we are Thine. We give ourselves to Thee.

Amen. Amen.

O God of sea and land,
>   Whose majesty we have seen in the blazing noon of mountain peaks,
>>   and in the afternoon sand against the ocean's blue,
>>   and in the shadows of evening spread across
>>>   a summer world of peaceful lawns against the lakes:
>   How eagerly now we wait You in this house we have made with hands!

O God, for every moment of healing peace and strengthening vision
>   with which You have blessed us in these days, we praise Your Name!
>   But we kneel most especially, Lord, grateful for this place that
>>   is our spirit's home.

We thank You that here amid this simple beauty we can gather
>   from home and office, and all the far places.

We thank You that here we can stand together, no longer as lone men and
>   women,
>   nor as separate families, but as the whole family of God:
>   Your people in this community, bringing all that we are—
>>   all our hopes and our faith, all our doubts and our questions—
>   to hear a Word from God, to be healed of our diseases,
>>   and saved from our weakness,
>>>   and lifted up from our loneliness, and given the faith with which
>>>>   to live life bravely and victoriously.

On this day of summer's ending and another year's opening out before us,
>   we remember how great is the need of this family of faith for You.
>   So much there is that needs to be done,
>   so many in this city who've not yet heard the call of Christ,
>   so many brokenhearted who need to be comforted,
>   so many seeking who have not found, so many troubled who need Your
>>   help!

Lord, they're all "our people."
>   They are the parish You have given us to care for.
>   And beyond this city are the soldiers of the Church—the shock troops—
>   teaching, and preaching, and healing
>   in every corner of the Earth where Christ has sent them.
>   And they are our teachers, our doctors, our preachers.
>>   They are part of us, and we of them!

O make us equal to the demands on us.
Make us a people ready to heed the call and do the work that we must
    do.

Lord, bless each member of this company!
    Help us to be disciples as were the twelve of old!
    Bless the teachers and the leaders of this company, Your Church,
    that they may come to their work with quickened spirits and high
        hopes.
    And bless our ministers, that they may be God's men—
        humble, brave, compassionate men.

Hear us, as in the silence we each pray for what we know we need.
In the Name of the One Who can do all things for those who love Him.

                        Amen.

O God, unto Whom even in the primeval dawn of time,
 men lifted up their hands in prayer,
 and Who has led men in all the ages since—whether in Roman cathedral,
  or Eastern mosque, or Hindu temple, or in New England meetinghouse—
 to offer thanks and praise to You whatever name they spoke:
 We, too, would join that wondrous cloud of witnesses to worship You
  and praise Your Name.

O glorious Lord of life, Who has such strange power to draw us to Your house
 when Sabbath comes:
 Each week the bells beckon—and we come!
 Each week something grows within to make us love this House the
  more—
  some word that helps, some prayer that speaks our heart,
  some new meaning, or some vision, that makes us see.

O God, for the very walls of this place we thank You.
 For her organ and her choir, for her pulpit and her table,
 for her plain New England beauty that opens up our spirits toward
  Your Spirit
 and makes this hour our hour of hope and help!

For the privilege of standing up among Christian friends
 to sing great hymns of faith, we thank You, Lord.
For the privilege of reading the Bible together as a people,
 we thank You, Lord.
For the privilege of prayer spoken silently in our hearts
 and aloud for us all to hear, we thank You, Lord.
For the privilege of preaching, for Your Word speaking to teach and to tell,
 to salve and to save, we thank You, Lord.
And especially for Christ, and for those who are our brothers in the
 covenant of faith, we give You glad and grateful thanks.

We worship You, we bow before You, we seek You—
 so that, by Your grace, our lives in the world may be strong,
  and good, and brave, and true:

We Sing Joy, Lord!

That our family lives may be homes of love,
   that our cities and our nation may be seats of justice, and
   that our offices and factories may be places of high purpose.
We worship You so that all of life may be lifted up to You and touched
      with eternity.
We pray for the concerns of life that need Your blessing—
   The homes of our friends where trouble is,
   the decisions of the nation where uncertainty is,
   and the personal concerns that each one knows.

O God, Whose way is to meet men in whatever need is theirs,
   to hear their faintest cry for help:
   Hear now our prayer, and accept all that we are and all that we bring.
      In the Name of Your Son and our Saviour, Jesus Christ.

Amen.

O God of this day in summer when the rain comes down as a dew from
        heaven,
    and the air is warm, and the grass is green,
    and the land is lush, and the birds sing,
    and there is a glow on everything:
The heart of Your people sings a song of praise
    for the wealth and the wonder of all these days.
We sing joy, Lord, because You are our joy.
We sing hope, Lord, because You are our hope.
We sing faith, Lord, because You are the One we believe in.
We sing love, Lord, because You are love. You showed us love, in Jesus.
    You gave us love, in Jesus.
    And all the rest You gave us, too, O Lord, in Jesus—faith, hope, joy.

Thanks for everything, God. Thanks for the summer sun.
Thanks for the patterns of clouds upon the hills.
Thanks for the stillness above the mountain tree line.
Thanks for the rolling surf across the white sands of the sea.
Thanks for the wind in full sails,
        for the whack of a golf ball down the course,
        for the long ride down of a surfboard on the sea,
        for the pounding hoofs of a good horse along the trail,
        for the tug of a northern on the line,
            and the dip of a paddle in the lake. And for tall pines,
            and clear stars, and for the Great Spirit—Your Holy Spirit—
                brooding over quiet waters.
        And for a change of pace, and the gift of peace,
        and for the healing of the heart, and a new look at life.
Thanks for the summer, Lord.
    And thanks for Sunday in the summer.
    And for all the people who have crowded here, because it's still Your
        day,
    and they love You still—and they love each other
    and want to stand here together,
        praying, believing, singing, hearing Your Word,
    and going out from this place to change the world.

O God, go with us! Make the world over!
>Change relationships through us; heal hurt hearts through us;
>comfort weary spirits through us; redeem the waiting world through us
>>by the power of Christ. Christ within us, Christ before us,
>>Christ in battle, Christ in triumph.

O Jesus, Saviour,
>let Your salvation reach out to touch Viet Nam.
>Let it save the lives of soldiers.
>Let it silence the guns of Sinai, and teach aggressors that they
>>who take the sword shall perish by the sword.
>Let Your salvation hold close every sick, sorrowing,
>>seeking, or sighing soul.

And most of all, we see our own salvation is, O Christ, in Thee!

Amen.

Prayers When Your Soul Is Sad

O, Sad Saviour,
> Who came not to condemn the world but to save the world—
> Carpenter from Nazareth, Prophet from the hills, Friend of sinners,
> Who looked upon the city of the prophets and wept over her,
> and then rode in, a King, to take the capital and make it Yours:

On this day of radiant sunlight,
> with palm branches fluttering like flags
> along the triumphal Victor's way,
> we see through the crowds and cries, Your tears;
> we feel the aching in Your heart on this day
>> when triumph turned to tragedy, when disciples became defectors,
> and our King was called a criminal.

Help us see that victory in life is not always won
> on the battlefields of history,
> that much more than prevailing before the crowds
> is prevailing in the secret heart where God alone can see—
> prevailing against temptation, against despair, against fear.
> Let this day of palms tell us over again Who our King really is;
>> Who He is Whom we hail and obey.
> And Lord, let us not be among those who turn from You!
> Let us not be traitors to Christ's high cause.
> Help us to stay by His side all through His last dark week.

O God, we want so much to do something for our Saviour.
> So much we want to tell Him how we feel.
> So much we want to honor Him for all His love.
> So much we want to cry out: He is ours! Our Christ. Our King. Our
>> Commander.
>> And we are His—and we love Him and we'll live for Him
>> and die for Him if we must!

Make us faithful in this week of walking the pilgrim way,
> this week of searching and of seeking,
> this week of deepening down in discipline and devotion—

Look to Jesus—He Will Listen!

gathering with the faithful company in a room above
    for the last loving meal together;
walking the hard road to the cross to wait through the dark hours
    for Christ's last cries.
And then, in the blush of Easter morning, at the early tomb,
    to find Him Risen, and know again that God has won,
    that death and evil at last are done,
    and that life is the truth—the Life Christ gives!

                      Amen.

Gracious Father, Whose look is one of love upon Your children—
    frail children of the Earth, weak men needing to be made strong,
    frightened men needing to find faith, and lost men needing to see the
        light—
glory do we sing to You! Glory in Immanuel's land,
    because Your kindness is from everlasting to everlasting,
    and Your forgiveness endures to all generations!
O Lord Jesus! Our generation needs that forgiveness!
        Our generation needs that strength, and faith, and light.
    And I need it, Lord, And this people needs it. All of them.
    All of us, with heads bent low before You now,
    hungry for a Word from You, waiting for a Word of hope, to help.

Good Christ, look at the girl who finds it so hard to see the way
    ahead for her, who has lost her way before she's even found it.
        Look at another one who has promised her life to You, and
    wants so much to stand upon the Rock of Ages sure and certain forever.
        Look at the widow, walking her lonely way through the
    valley of the shadow, wondering if the sun will ever shine for her.
        Look at the young man who in the midst of tragedy has
    found a meaning for his life.
    They're each Your children, Lord.
    They're each here today, looking for an answer.
    Don't let them go away with empty hands, or empty hearts.
    Don't let them say there is no Christ for them today,
    no Lord with hand to heal them, nor with love enough to comfort
        them,
    nor with light enough to guide them!

Be sufficient for us all, O Lord.
    We'll never make it through the week ahead without Your
    armor to protect us, Lord; without the guarding of Your angel hosts
    about us; and without the victory songs our brothers sing still
    ringing in our ears!

Remember, Lord, the troubled and the grieving and the sick.
Remember the lost ones who just can't seem to find their way,
    and hide themselves behind false fronts! We've all done that!

Help them see that in Christ they can find themselves.
Be with the ones mowed down with marriage problems.
Heal their hurt and hate, O Lord, and open up the way for love.
And look on those who walk with death, and let them know they're not
      alone.

O Lord, the Victor over death and sin and suffering,
    and Who alone wipes all tears away:
    Be our life and hope today, and all this week,
    because You love us, Lord!

        Amen.

O Christ of the Cross, Who had so much to do with death,
    and with sickness, and with sin;
    Who faced every day these principalities and powers,
    and Who calls the world again and again to walk that way:
        It is so hard to be a Christian! We believe in You, Lord!
        We Know God loved the world through You.
        We know You died for our sins—
        those subtle sins we find it so hard to confess, and
        especially the ones such as spiritual pride, and hardness of heart,
        and not loving the brethren.
    You even died for these, as well as for our immorality,
        our selfishness, our cruelty, and our neglect.
    And we know, Lord, about Your forgiveness, and Your compassion,
        and Your sheer and wondrous grace.
    They mean everything to us!
Lord, we really do believe! We're "true blue," in faith.
    We just think You're great! We're all for You! We know the words.
    We have the answers. We know the way we ought to go.
What we need, Lord, is for You to help our unbelief!

How can it be, Lord, that we should know it all but somehow not know
        You?
How can it be that we should have the answers but somehow fail to live the
        life?
Lord, that's hard. I mean, really living the life. Living it with You.
    Going where You go, walking where You walk, saying what You say.
You were such a threat to the entrenched power structure of church and
        state
    that they combined to kill You.
    But nobody wants to kill us, Lord. We're so tame we don't threaten or
        disturb anybody.
    Forgive us, Lord.
    Help us to be brave—like You, Who carried a cross.
    We don't really want to carry a cross, or deny ourselves,
        or lay down our lives for our friend.
    When we are faced with the call to lose our lives,
        we justify, we rationalize, and make it so easy for ourselves
        to make our witness just by talking, and not by doing.

    Help us to believe, Lord, all the way!

Make us Your witnesses. Make us Your soldiers. Make the Church the
chariot of the Gospel, telling it far and wide to young and old,
rich and poor, sick and well that Jesus Christ is Lord,
and that He calls us all to repent and believe!
In Your great Name we pray.

Amen.

O Holy Spirit, Wind of Heaven,
Who steals upon the hearts of men like a thief in the night,
possessing unsuspecting lives with power,
until a host of Spirit-driven men go blazing a path of faith across the
Earth,
crying out that He Who was dead is alive again,
that those who were weak are strong again, and those who were
lost are found again:
All praise and glory to You, O Lord most high! Wondrous is Your
Name, O God,
and marvelous are Your works to the children of men!

Before that Spirit Presence, brooding over the face of our world,
touching a life here, filling a soul with glory there—
we kneel in awe and thankfulness.
When all real inspiration, all true gifts of genius,
all the depths of understanding, and all the transformed lives
are the strange surpassing fruit of that amazing Spirit,
we cannot help but give our praise and thanks to You!

O, give us that Spirit, Lord.
Pour it out upon Your Church where'er it gathers.
But especially here, where our heads are bowed and our lives laid open.
Lord, if any have come expecting to find no blessing here,
no healing for burdened minds, no lifting of weary shoulders,
no joy for saddened hearts, no new life for jaded spirits—
if some have come really expecting to go away from this house of God
as they came, unhealed and unhelped—
Surprise them, O God! Surprise them with the gift of Your Spirit for their
lives!
Help them look up, and laugh, and sing again.
Make their hearts leap for joy, and their spirits drink in the beauty
of a world that was made for them.
And touch them with faith, O God!
Especially seek out here, Lord, the lives of the young,
and win them for Jesus.

There's a Wind Blowing—a Spirit of Hope

Let some souls here today, hear the old eternal cry,
    this time to them, calling: "Come, and follow Me!"

Because of our hope in Your living Spirit,
    we make bold, O Lord, to pray for the Church,
    that its mission be endowed with power
    and its life blessed with the unseen rewards of the Spirit.
Remember its families everywhere,
    and blest be the tie that binds them to the Church.
Bind all the families of the Earth, O Lord, into one great family of faith,
    that we may be one in Christ,
        and do His works with power, to the honor and glory of His holy
            Name!

Amen.

O Jesus, Lord, Who alone is King of kings, and Lord of lords:
We're the poor souls of Earth who, even while we know You,
have set up other gods and bowed down to them!
O Lord, ride into our lives today and master our souls, we pray!
Scale the walls of our indifference! Batter our hearts with Your love!
Come, subdue our rebellious spirits, and make us Yours forever and
forever!

You know, Lord, that we are part of the brokenness
of this hurt and hating world that cries to You for help.
Our world is at war because we've let ourselves share in the
anger that makes for war.
There is no peace because we have not loved peace enough.
There is no brotherhood of man because we have not remembered who
our brother is!
And there is no victory of faith because we have not put faith first in
life.

O God, take away the things that keep us from being the Christians
we were called to be!
If it be success—make us failures! If it be prosperity—make us poor!
If it be power—make us weak! If it be this world's wisdom—make us
fools!
For Christ's sake.

Master of men Who knew no fear,
Who loved every man yet was not weak,
Who spoke the truth though it hurt to speak,
Who cared for all yet was out-cast in return,
Who bore the cross but did not cry in pain:
Help us be brave.
Help us love You gladly as men ought to love.
Help us serve You purely with no mar or stain.
Help us give self freely, as You gave all to us.

There's a Light Shining to Show the Way Home

And Lord, bless our town, our country, and the nations
    with the peace, and hope, and laughter that
    is Yours alone to give, and without which they cannot live.
So, Lord, Whose joy we hear in the singing of the birds,
    and see in the glory of the sunrise:
    Grant us to be joyful all the day long, to be glad in Your love,
    radiant in Your inner peace, and eager with each day's promise.
    That in the splendor of the morning
    or the quiet wonder of the evening,
        we may sing Your praises forever and forever.

Amen.

O Man from Nazareth, Who came, turning darkness into the dawning
     and dispelling the shadows of night from every fearful heart
     until Heaven's light shone full upon them:
     We wonder at the love so great that Lazarus lived,
     and that all men live when they know You!
     How strange Your coming was! No man ever spoke as You did speak.
     No man ever stood strong as You did always stand.
     Nor did any man command the powers of darkness as You did with but
          a word.
     Death's legions fled before Your face,
     and the hosts of evil cowered at the majesty of Your grace!

O Saviour of the world, Who rides the chariots of Heaven
     and marshals the companies of the angels in Your camp:
     Dawn comes at your behest, and stars light the night because You set
          them shining.
     But even more, our lives are lived because You are Lord of life.
     Your will is life—and hope and joy, and power and peace—
     and love and faith are Yours to give.

O Lord, the enemy of disease and death,
     Who carries in Your bosom every hurt thing of Earth,
     caring for the weak and overburdened,
     lifting the lost and the despairing, seeking the sorrowing and the sick:
     Conquer the darkness that seeks to shroud our souls, O Lord!
     Defeat our little despairs, lift up our weeping heads,
     and give us eyes to see and ears to hear,
     until the dazzling dawn of Heaven's light spreads glory round our lives,
     and the music of the spheres comes singing across the river its
          alleluia songs!

Lord, we are Martha's and Mary's a hundred times over!
     All of us have known sorrow's pain and fear's despair.
     And yet we are here, in this place of faith, because in
     ways we cannot say, we have found Your healing light upon us.
     Your hand has wiped our tears away, Your arm has circled round our
          shoulders,
     and we have found the blessing of a peace that passes all understanding.

O let Your peace rest upon all who need it here today!
     Calm the harried hearts that are in our midst.
     Comfort the sorrowing who live among us in loneliness.
     Strengthen the weak who have no strength but You.
     Heal the sick who can have no life except in You.
     Let the victory of Your love fill our hearts with gratitude and joy,
     with courage and with hope. And may it send us to the world as
     messengers of the King, proclaiming the glory and gladness of the
     world's Redeemer, Who reigns for ever and ever.

                              Amen.

O Light of the world,
>   Who dawns upon the day like thunder from the east,
>   spreading across the earth the magnificence of morning's gold;
>   Who sets the night aglow with the rising of the moon
>   and the far-off flickering of the stars.
O Lord, Who turns every darkness into dawning,
>   Who lines every cloud of life with silver,
>   Who takes the weeping hearts of men and makes them laugh again,
>   and lets us sing when once we thought no song would ever pass our lips
>   again!

What miracles of the human spirit are Yours, O God.
>   There is so much that seems so often without hope to us;
>   so much that hangs heavy on our minds;
>   so much that is a burden and a heartache to us, Lord.
>   And then You come on wings of love and say:
>   "Let not your heart be troubled . . . peace be unto you.
>   In the world ye shall have tribulation, but be of good cheer,
>   I have overcome the world!"
O Jesus Christ, You are indeed the light of the world, and
>   in You is no darkness at all!

All thanks to You, Lord, for this mystery with which You preserve
>   us from the darkness that our own hearts make.
>   Thanks be to You for turning into such joy the labors of life that
>   would be intolerable burdens upon us except for You.
You are our life, O Lord.
>   You are our hope. You are our salvation!

Even as You have delivered us from all the little darknesses of our lives
>   into the glorious liberty and light of Jesus Christ,
>   save our world, O God!
We are not the only ones who need You.
The people of the whole Earth walk in darkness.
>   Let them see the great light!
>   Let them find eyes to see and ears to hear!

Let them know the thrill of Your glory in the morning;
    and at night the benediction of Your peace, which passes
      understanding.

O Lord, destroy the darkness that sickness brings.
    Banish the fears that apprehension creates.
    Lift the burdens that grow heavy with dull routine,
and fill us with light, that Christ may shine in us where'er we go.
    Lord, we give ourselves to You.
    We give our faith, our strength, our hope to You!

> *O Light that followest all my way,*
>   *I yield my flickering torch to Thee.*
> *My heart restores its borrowed ray*
>   *That in Thy sunshine's blaze its day*
> *May brighter, fairer be!*

Amen.

Prayers for the Longing Life

O Alpha and Omega, Beginning and the End;
> You Who were at our beginning and will be at our ending, too;
> You from Whom all life has come, and to Whom all life goes:
>> We come to You, Lord.
> The days pass, and closer yet draws on that unknown day—
> the day that comes like a thief in the night,
>> when life in this land of Earth shall end and new life shall
>>> come,
>> and every veil of dark shall drop away
>> and we shall see You, Our God, and know You, and live our
>>> lives with You.

Help us to be ready, Lord.
> Let not the day of death be a thing of fear for us.
> Let it be instead the coronation day for us!
>> A day of triumph, a day of music, a day of gladness and of
>>> singing,
>> when Heaven's chorus shall break into shouts of holy joy.
>> and the cross shall win its final victory of life
>> over every dark and dead and sinful thing in us.

O God our Lord, take us, we pray, today,
> up into high mountains of the spirit
> where we can see beyond the limits of this world,
> and find the vision of a great world coming—
>> of God's Kingdom fulfilled and complete, and pure and glorious,
> in that place above known to us as Heaven.
Let Heaven be the hunger of our hearts, O Lord.
> Let it be for us that dear and far-off land to which we go.

And Lord, carry on their way, we pray,
> every traveling soul of men that looks that way.
> Bear up the way-worn, unburden the heavy-laden,
> journey with the singing and the hopeful.
And make us, we pray, a company of pilgrim people
> traveling toward a land we love!

Prayer in Sorrow

And among the pilgrim band,
>   remember the friend who has suffered a disappointment,
>   strengthen the one who fights the tempter,
>   and bear up the ones overcome by sickness.
Make us men with a vision, Lord;
>   men whose home is not here, but who name another land as their
>   own—
>   the land of hope and glory, where the broken is healed,
>   the sinful redeemed and the separated reconciled,
in the love of Him Who is our Saviour and Redeemer, Jesus Christ.

Amen.

O Lord Jesus, I want to know You—all of us want to know You!
    It's Advent time: the eager, angel time; the waiting time.
    The time of silent snow and December nights.
    The time of still stars and singing from afar.
    The miracle time when even unbelieving men steal close to the stall
        to see if any of it's true at all.

Even we Christians forget, Lord.
    All us churchmen who are there so regularly
    and take part so faithfully, even we forget, Lord.
    And our faith fails, and grows uncertain,
    and we do things we never dreamed we'd do.
        We sin, Lord. We falter and we fall. We do not answer to the
        call.

Because, Lord, it's hard to see You there—
    to see the way You answer prayer.
    It's hard to know if You're for real,
    and if Your joy and power we can ever feel.
Help us find the way today, O Lord.
Help us have Advent eyes, and eager ears, and hopeful hearts.
Help us to expect You, and look for You, and not doubt or ever despair.
    And if some of us are struggling, Lord, to keep to the high road,
    to walk the hills and not the hollows, to be pure and good and not
    evil follow:

Have mercy on us! Make our faith strong, and our love pure,
    and our lives honorable, and our secrets open—to You.
Let us be good soldiers. Help us fight to the end, and all good defend.

Bless the soldiers, Lord, on battlefields of blood.
Bless the enemy for the Christmas truce.
Bless the politicians—and make them statesmen.
Bless the college students.
Bless the unwed mothers.
Bless the troubled, lonely lovers.

Prayers When Your Life's in Trouble

Bless the sick and those who grieve, let them healing now receive.
And bless us in our family wide,
and bless the tie that binds our broken, hopeful hearts in Christmas
love.

Amen. Amen.

O God, what shall we render to You for Your benefits toward us?
With what shall we come before the Lord,
and bow ourselves before the high God?
Shall we offer You nothing but the forms of faith—
nothing but the arid duties of an inconvenient and
grudging devotion?
Shall we come before You with offerings, with calves of a year old?
Will the Lord be pleased with thousands of rams, or with
ten thousand rivers of oil?

O God, You have shown us what is good
and what the Lord in His love requires of us:
to be just men, to be merciful men, and to be humble men
who are not too proud to walk with God.
O Son of Man, Carpenter of Nazareth, Friend of sinners:
have You drawn near on the road of life to walk with us,
and found us too proud, too concerned with our own affairs to walk
with You?
Have You rested by some watering place and found us there,
and invited us to be Your companions on the way,
only to have us turn our backs and look away
because we had more important things to do—sales meetings to attend,
business deals to close, inventories to take, important speeches to
make—
and no time left for the business of the Master?

O Jesus Christ, so full of accountings our lives are!
Sales slips of a hundred kinds, bills for services rendered,
orders for the goods of life we need,
long tapes from the market with endless figures,
neat columns of what we owe to men:
Have You no bill to render us?
Comes there no time of accounting unto You?
What do we owe You, O Lord? A dollar or two?
Or ten, or fifty, or five hundred?
Not enough? You want everything, Lord? All we have? Our lives?
Can we hold nothing back, O Christ?

Not just some little thing to call our own?
Some harmless indulgence, some bad habit, some sensual sin,
      some little pride, a touch of vanity perhaps at how important we
      know we really are?
Not even this? O Master of men, Your price is high! You want our lives.
You want the very secret of our success—our confidence, our pride.
You want our hearts, our love, until no gift will be too great to give,
      no life too brave and bold to live, nor any humiliation too deep
           to dare!

Batter our hearts this day, O Christ,
until with conscience troubled, and peace disturbed, and all pride shattered
we may stand at last, Your sons: No longer afraid, no longer uncertain,
      but ready for the call, to serve in love our Lord and Saviour,
      our Master and Friend, Jesus Christ.

> *Nothing in our hands we bring,*
>   *Simply to Thy Cross we cling;*
> *Naked, come to Thee for dress,*
>   *Helpless, look to Thee for grace:*
> *Foul, we to the fountain fly,*
>   *Wash us, Saviour, or we die!*

Amen.

O Lord, with angels and archangels, and all the company of Heaven,
  we laud and magnify Your holy Name, ever more praising You, and
      saying—
  Holy, Holy, Holy, Lord God of Hosts, Heaven and earth are full of
  Your Glory—Glory be to You, O Lord most High!
Lord, for the sending of this Saviour we praise You.

Such a wonder it is, Lord, that a child should be our Saviour;
  that a baby born of unknown parents
  and raised in an insignificant city should be our Saviour.

For we are so accustomed to saving ourselves:
  We make it our business to be equal to every situation.
  The whole world, Lord, all our experience,
  teaches us that our calling is to appear confident,
  to be masters of our fate, to live by bluster and assurance.

But Lord, underneath, where no one else can see,
  we are not masters of our destiny, we are not certain,
  not strong and confident and booming men.
We are little men, lost men, lonely men.
  We're even ready to bid a little child welcome as our Saviour.

God, if He can give us peace, which we have never found in life;
  if He can give us hope, so that despair cannot destroy us;
  if He can give us faith, so that "neither death, nor life, nor angels,
      nor principalities, nor powers, nor things present, nor things to
          come"
  nor anything, can separate us from You:
Then we will welcome this child with all the honor human hearts can bestow,
  and all the longing hope that the lives of harassed humanity knows.

Prayer When You're Afraid

O Saviour God, Holy Child, before Whom kings and shepherds
 and Your own family knelt: We kneel and ask Your blessing today.
 Take away our pride.
 Forgive our foolishness.
 Humble our hearts.
 And if You will,
   Save us, we pray!

   Amen.

O Jesus, our Saviour and our Lord,
    Who once walked high roads with twelve
        to tell them they were Your friends,
    and Who walks now the whole world's highways
        in company of any man whose heart
        is open to take You as his friend:
Don't pass by, we pray, this house's door,
    for the lamps are lit,
        the table of our heart is spread,
        and we wait for You.
"*Marana Tha!* Even so, come, Lord Jesus!"

O come to us, whose hearts are aching today
    and whose spirits are a vale of tears.
    Touch us with Your hands that touched so many into life,
        and draw back the curtains of our darkness
        until light shines, and morning comes for us!
    O sometimes, Lord, we're so alone.
        Sometimes our hearts have secrets that we cannot tell.
            Only You can know.
    Sometimes our feet lift like lead in life
        because of dark within, not yet dispelled.
    Help us to be whole. Make us to be strong.
        Don't let us fear, for You are near.

Wipe away, O Lord, every tear from our eyes,
    and let there be no more sorrow,
        nor crying,
        nor pain, any more.
    Let the former things be passed away,
    and let all things for us be made new,
        with You.

Prayer When You're Lonely

For love's sake,
and life's sake,
and the Gospel's sake,
Whose bearers we are
when our lives show afar
            the great God that You are!

            Amen.

O God! We cry to You across the dark emptiness of space.
    We rocket round the Earth,
    we send our spacecraft probing like fragmentary fingers
    out into the darkness toward the moon, toward Venus, and toward
        Mars.
But somewhere within is always the cry: *GOD! WHERE ARE YOU?*
    Are You out there? Are You in the heavens,
    Farther away than we can ever imagine, and yet closer and nearer than
        we know?

Where, God, and how? Will we ever join You there?
    Is there some place, some day, where we will know You,
        where we will see You face to face?
What is Heaven, Lord?
What does it mean that Christ the Lord rose victorious over death,
    and brought captivity captive, and opened up the road for us to *live?*
Teach us, today, O Lord. Make firm our faith,
    and kindle within us the deep desire to follow You not alone through
        life,
    but even through the doors of death and out into the eternal dawn of
        life beyond.

Teach us to love Jesus, to trust Him, to take Him for our Friend
    and to hold His hand, and walk His way, and find Him our daily hope
        and help.
Help us to choose for Him,
    to cast in our lot on His side,
    to become His men today and tomorrow—for now and forever.

O High King of Heaven, Whose promise is life eternal:
    Make it a promise also to the world!
    Redeem the time, O Lord!
    Redeem it from anger and fear, from prejudice and hate, from war and
        death.
    Reach out Your healing hand to touch a troubled world,
        and heal sick lives and hearts.

Prayers for the Seeking Soul

And show in countless concrete ways that You are here,
    where we are, and not just out there.
    You're here where we need You and where the world needs You—
        right now, today, always, and here, near—driving away our fear.
        Thank you.

        Amen.

O God, Who dwells in the secret place of the most high
    and Who is the very shadow of the Almighty;
    God of the dark mystery of great cathedral and wayside church;
    and God Whose mystery is the Earth itself, and the changing seasons,
    and the infinite stars, beyond man's reason:
        In awe and reverent silence we steal into this sacred place
        and bend the knee, and bow the heart, and ask a blessing.

O Lord, like Samuel of old we wait to hear Your voice.
    Speak Lord, for Your servants hear You.
    Speak to our senses. Speak to our souls.
    Tell us Who You are! Tell us how we can see You.
    Tell us how we can serve You.

O God, we come so casually into Your house—
    clattering and chattering,
    making the holy house hum with our endless talk.
    Oh, we mumble and fumble,
    and forget to pray as we approach Your church on Sabbath day!

What if You were here, God?
What if, in mystery and power, You were here this hour?
What if, like Isaiah, we looked up to see You—Your real and
    very presence, filling this place.
    In fear and trembling we would stand.
    And such a hush would fall o'er this place that no one would dare to
        rush,
        but silently, in solemn wonder, enter here to ask Your grace and
            love.
    We'd have no trouble praying, Lord.
    Every heart would be turned to You,
    and not a mind would wander, nor any thought stray away!

Make our prayer to be so today!
    Lift up our hearts! We lift them up unto the Lord.
    Hear our prayer—for ourselves, for new faith,
        for deeper dedication, for our friends in need.
    Make us a company of men who know the Master
    and who live for Him with faith, and fear, and loving wonder, here.

Amen.

O Lord, for these my brothers and my sisters of the way, I pray.
    We want to come
    as at the altar fires of the centuries,
    to gather at the Table spread by Christ, the Lord of the centuries;
    to approach with halting hearts unto the Holy of holies,
        there to be fed with the Bread of life,
        there to be made whole by the Lord of life,
        and there to drink the cup of salvation
            and be made clean and good and pure again,
            until the time of parting comes.
    And then to go out into the world that is waiting,
        with the flags of the faith flying,
        and the cross of Christ blazing,
        and the love of the Lord shining in our lives.

O Holy Spirit, Who is brooding over this town,
    quickening many hearts
    and bringing a new day of power for the Church:
We pray for our comrades of the cross in all our sister Churches.
    Especially do we pray for their pastors—
                for the pastors of the Catholic churches,
                for the pastors of the Congregational churches,
                for the Lutheran pastors,
                for the Covenant pastors, and for all the rest.

We pray, too, a special prayer
    for those fighting for life in the hospital,
    and for those devastated by sudden death.

Lord, as we come to the Table so tentatively and so timidly,
    so well aware of the sin that makes us unworthy,
    we bring You all our concerns—
        we lay them at Your feet.
            Remember the young people fighting for faith.
            Remember the old people, treasuring their life.
            And we lay before You India and Pakistan,
                and South America, and Viet Nam, and Germany.
            And every torn and troubled country.

Prayers at Communion

Heal the world, O Lord,
>and make the Church in every land
>a witness to that healing,
>and to Your love in Jesus Christ, Who died for us.
>May the blood of Christ, and the blessing of His compassion,
>>be upon us all for ever and ever,
>>>world without end.

Amen.

O Lord Jesus, God among men, friend of every man,
    strong stranger with the healing hand,
    face of calm and courage bronzed by the wind and sun of human life
    yet shining with the radiance of a life Divine:
We lift to You our eyes,
    believing that in this simple, sacred place
    Your Spirit's life can shine,
    and seeking, faithful men really can see Jesus.

We would see Jesus, Lord.
    We would look up and feel a presence,
    and hear a Word, and see Your face.
    In the quiet of communion, help our hearts be right
    so that our ears may hear, and our eyes may see.
    Let us see You in the gathering of the deacons round the Holy Table.
    Let us see You in the faces of our friends
        as we sing of the "tie that binds" when this service ends.
    And let us feel You in their hands as they hold ours.
    Let us all know we have been with Christ today.

We need so much today! We need to confess our sin.
    We need to be forgiven. We need healing for our bodies,
    and peace for our spirits, beyond all understanding.
Come now, in this quiet hour, to give that healing,
    and to hear our confession, and to make us whole.
        Even so, come, Lord Jesus . . . now, in the silence. . . .

And Lord, not for ourselves alone would we pray.
    For the whole Church, struggling in Eastern Europe against official
        atheism,
        fighting prejudice and persecution in South Africa,
        facing terror and constant threat of life in our own Deep South,
        and all about us battling against indifference to win men's
        hearts for Christ.

For our country, too, we pray—
    that she may never give in to the cries of fear,
        nor fail in fortitude.
        But stand with Christian compassion as a great nation
            seeks to lift the burdens of poverty,
            and to make ours a people rich in courage and concern,
            a flaming fire of hope across a darkened world!
And for our own comrades of the cross we offer all our prayers and love
        today:
    For the binding up of every human wound,
    and for making us a true family of faith—
    forgiving one another, caring for one another,
    and serving one another and the world. In Jesus' Name.

                            Amen.

Almighty God, Maker of heaven and Earth: Beautiful is the world today,
    blue is the sky today, glorious is the sun today,
        full are our hearts today.
Thank You for such a day as this!
Thank You for letting us be alive to walk out in a day like this!
Thank You for gathering us here,
    a glad company of Your people on a day like this!

You have made it all, O God,
    The Earth is Yours,
    The sun, the sky, the fields, and forests;
        the lawns and lakes of this land all are Yours.
    And we are Yours. Every one of us.

You made us, Lord. You had such hopes and dreams for us,
    You had such a great destiny for us.
    How we have disappointed You!
    How we have hurt and angered You!
        By our selfishness, by our willfulness, by our pride,
        by our foolish arrogance that thinks that we control the world
        and that we control our lives,
            that we can manipulate others' lives, that we need no one except
                ourselves.
O Holy God, Whose heart we hurt so often by our great promises
    and our poor performance,
    by our church piety and our daily unrighteousness:
        Hear our confession, and forgive, we pray!

O Lord, we deserve darkness from You,
    and death from You, and eternal punishment from You.
But that's not what You have given. You loved us. You loved the world.
    You sent Your Son to save us—to rescue us from ourselves,
    from our sin. In Him You even died for us!
How can we accept such a great gift, O God?
    How can we take from One Who gives so much?
    Only by Your promises do we come.

Prayers When You Need Forgiveness

"Come unto Me," You said, "and I will give you rest."
"He who believes will be saved."

O Lord Jesus Christ, Son of God, Saviour of men:
    We do come to You.
        Save us! Forgive us! Gather us close to You.
        Show us the way. Help us hold high the cross,
            to be soldiers of the Lord, to love the lost as You love them,
    and to win the world You died to save.

O Shepherd of the sheep, hold us all in Your love
    and help us to live for the Lord Christ our Saviour.

                Amen.

O God most holy,
     with Whom a thousand years is but a day,
     and before Whom the nights and days of a million centuries
          pass unending–day unto day, and night unto night!
     Time, like an ever-rolling stream, bears all its sons away.
     But You are the same yesterday, today, and forever.
          You never change. Only we change.
     We with our erring, fickle ways;
     we with our petty passions, our little loyalties, and our many moods.

O Lord Jesus Christ,
     Child of Bethlehem, Son of Nazareth,
     King of Jerusalem, and Lord of the Earth:
     Have mercy on us, Your weaker brethren,
          who bend with the winds of life and flow with its tides.
     You alone offer hope of a second chance.
     You alone write "forgiven!" across the ledger of our lives,
          and send us on our way with the great cry:
          "Go, and sin no more!"
     We do not want to sin any more, Lord.
     We want to start again. I mean, all over again.
     We want to have a new life in a new year.
     We want to have the pages of our days that are passed turned over
          to the pages of great new beginnings–
          the kind of beginning Christ gives.

O God of today and tomorrow,
     God Who makes every dawn to rise,
     and touches the hills with the finger of the morning,
     and causes every evening to come with the shades of night pulled down,
     and darkness to cover the deep with healing hands and restful sleep:
O God, prepare us for a new day, a new year, a new life coming,
     and for the chance to begin again–as new men.

We pray for forgiveness for all that is past,
     and for strength to meet new days and walk new ways.

Let it be with our Lord Christ that we live them,
and make them be days of victories over every weakness, every fear,
     every fault, and every failing that does beset us.
And look now upon our comrades of the cross,
who in the days that are past have gone on to the other side
     to fight in heaven's legions.
And may the hosts of Heaven guard the unseen way ahead for all of us
who would be warriors for our Saviour in the world!

                        Amen.

O God, Whose glory is the fanfare of shout and song across the Earth, where
    each new day comes up to wake the world;
        Whose breath is the west wind that blows the breeze of spring across
            our winter-weary land; and whose love is whole valleys blossoming
            into life, and the hills becoming green again, and the heart of
            man having hope again: This is Your world!
It belongs to You. The soil and the sea are Yours. And the sand and the sky
    are Yours.
Your hand holds it all. Your hand holds us. You are so great, and Your
    power is so great!

We see the miracle of Your mighty works in the world and we can only
    marvel.
    But when we see Your hand in human affairs,
    when we see Your power in Jesus Christ bringing love to lost lives
    and making men see the world and themselves in a whole new way;
    when we see the very hearts of men changed by Your power:
        We wonder if we should not have power, too!
        We wonder if a new light and a new life shouldn't be shining in
            us, too.
        We wonder if we shouldn't be counting for more in the cause,
        if we shouldn't more surely be bringing something great to the
            world,
            to the world we know—this little world of our own village
            and the bigger world of our whole city, this world of men
            and their machines, this world of people and their needs.

Are we missing something, God?
    Surely, Lord, the times they are a-changin'—
    they must be changing if the kingdom of our Lord and Christ is ever
        yet to come!
    Should we not be turning this world upside down for our Jesus,
        as our first-century fathers did before us?
    Should we not be changing things, Lord, in the power of Your love?

O God, if we've settled only for the forms of faith,
    stir up a questing in our lives, we pray.

Prayers When You're Looking for Reality

If we have followed only afar off, help us to draw near and learn the secret.
   Put into our hands, O Lord Jesus, the power to heal and help,
   to be conquerors in the conquest of life.
And Lord, if there are among us those who have felt beaten and battered
   in the battle of life, who are wounded and weary and defeated by the
          strife:
   Encourage them today, give them rest and relief on the way, and
   strength enough for the fray.

Especially we ask for the sick and the suffering, the lost and the lonely.
   And make us be all together, we pray, a people of power today—
   that here, among us, hearts may be healed, and lives lifted up,
   and hope and help given, and this company become indeed
   a communion of the saints and companions of the Saviour:
          With a song to sing, and a salvation to bring, and a word of hope
          to wing to the world, and all men in it. For Jesus' sake.

Amen.

O God, You never yet have turned Your back
    on anyone who needed You.
        Sometimes we have thought the skies were closed
        and that no ear was in Heaven to hear us,
        and we've wanted to chuck it all and say:
    "There is no prayer, and maybe there is no God!"
But in our heart of hearts we know that is not true.
    We know there is a truth—something real that needs to be revealed to us.
O help us see the point of prayer.
    Help us feel its power, and know that in this hour
    this prayer is heard—
    because, for lots of us, Lord, prayer together has been the most
        meaningless of our public exercises.

We confess it, Lord.
    We've only gone through the motions—
    listening to words that were not our own,
    bowing down our heads but not our hearts,
    and saying, when we are honest, that prayer leaves us cold,
    that it is not what we come for, anyway!
O God! What a cold company we've been! Where has the fire gone?
    Where is the deep spirit that in every age of the Church's history
        has brought men stealing into the throne room of the Most High,
        there to be lost in wonder, love, and praise?
What has happened to the human spirit among us?
    Is there no hunger for the Divine?
    Are we so jaded by all the jangling jingles of our TV time
        that there is no love left that can turn
        itself humbly unto God in prayer?

O send down Your Spirit, Lord!
    Make this a moment of meaning for us.
    If some are so distracted that they cannot seem to hear,
    still their rustling restlessness
    and let the quietness of the heart descend upon them now.

If some today impatiently wait for this moment to move on,
    and be over and done with,
    lay Your patient hand on them
    and let them be still and know that You are God!

Let us all be still, and speak You now to us in silence—
    healing all our hurts, binding up our wounds, and making each one
    strong for his work in the world this week.
Come, Lord, and make our worship real.
    If any has a special need, come close to meet it, Lord.
        And even if prayer be hard for us, make it swift and powerful for
            them.
    In Jesus' Name.

    Amen.

Prayers of the New Life

O Lord Jesus,
    Man of the hour in all the ages of human history,
    Man at the well when a woman came in need,
    Man in a million lives who brought from despair the victory,
    Man on Calvary's cross that all men might be freed:
We love You, and worship You, and adore You.
    We pledge our lives to You,
    we give our hearts to You,
    we commit to You our love, our hope, and our sacred honor.
        God, Who became man for us;
        Saviour, Who died once and for all on the lonely hill;
        Gracious Lord, Our Risen, Redeeming Friend
            for us—
            for now—
            and for eternity!

Come to us in our awful need,
    watch over us in our every deed,
make us pure and lovely within, without—
    with conscience clear, and a heart to shout
    that we are Yours
        and that we love You true,
        and no dark deed would we think or do!

Lord God, Who knows the secret of every heart,
        Who knows our sin from the very start:
    Come, cleanse our lives.
    Forgive us, please,
        as we bow down
        on bended knees.

And send us on our way, rejoicing, free,
    knowing we are Your children, even we!
And set free our world, O Lord. Bind the powers of darkness
    that seem sometimes to hold even nations in their grip.

We Know You, Lord, and We're Yours!

Redeem the lost and suffering countries of Southeast
Asia. Redeem our world at war. Redeem the lost, willful
lives of all world's men. Redeem the time, Lord.
     Come again, O God, and claim this world
     You died to save. And make us Your
     soldiers in that great cause.
          Even so come, Lord Jesus!

          Amen. Amen.

Dear God, this is Your Church.
>   We don't own it. You own us.
>   You called us to live Your life, to do Your work,
>   to see Your vision and dream Your dream.

If what we've talked about today is not Your will,
if it's not Divine but of the Devil—destroy it, Lord,
>   before we take one step.
>   Show us by some sign that it is wrong, all wrong!
>   But if it's right—God, help us *move!*
>   Help us move out and claim that future,
>   help us take our stand, and be the church
>   You put us here to be.

O Jesus Christ,
>   Who gave Your life away to show Your Church how it might live:
>   Don't let us be afraid of adventure.
>   Don't let us pale at the thought of giving away
>   more than we ever had before.
>   And don't let us have faint hearts when we are faced with
>   the chance to do something big,
>   something dangerous, something difficult.

Bind the fellowship together! Forge us like steel!
>   Make us a sword of the Spirit in Your hands.
>   Make us a blade of power for You to use.
>   Make us an oaken staff.

Help us to "travel on and still be stirred, by silent thought
>   or social word. By all our perils undeterred, Soldiers, pilgrim-staid!"

O God, on this day we pray for every comrade of the cross
>   Who companions not with us today because
>   he's sick in hospital or grieved in spirit.
>   Be, Lord, with each one in tender, healing comfort.
>   May they all, from sickness, suffering, or sorrow,
>   rise up and walk.
>   And may we, too, rise up and walk.
>   Let these bones live, Lord.

And let our lives be bright and shining beacons for You,
to this town and to this city and to the world—
every part of it: the hurt, bleeding part in battle,
and the affluent, unscathed part right here.
Lord, the whole world needs You—and needs us, too, serving in Your Name.

Amen.

O Jesus Christ, the Saviour of the world and our Saviour;
      Son of God and Son of Man, Who heard the cries of a troubled world
      and came Yourself to answer them: Hear our prayer today.

We come from a wearying world
      where the sounds of the streets have clamored in our ears,
      and the demands of desk and duty have drained our bodies,
      and the secret sorrows of the soul have made us sad,
      and the terrors of disjointed times have left us tense and troubled.
Out of the battering whirlwind of such a world,
      we come as once Elijah did,
      to a quiet place to hear the still, small voice of God.

O Jesus, Lord and Friend,
      tender and merciful Saviour Who is God among us:
      Stretch out Your hands to heal us.
      We have learned You are the One only Who can help us.
      You are the One Who, again and again,
      has touched us in the throng and press of life
      and said, "Peace, be still!"
      You are the One who has found us sick and broken,
      and lifted us up to life.
      You are the One Who has touched our blindness and made us see,
      and opened our ears to understand.
      When life was dark You made the sun to shine again,
      when burdens were heavy You made them light again,
      when doubts were deep You gave us faith again.
You Only have the words of eternal life.
You Only make the mornings magic, and life glorious, and love beautiful for
        us!
You Only are the One Who can bring God close,
      and make darkness of light, and turn sorrow into singing,
      and mourning into joy, and life into laughter!
      And we praise You for it. We honor You for it. We laud and magnify
        You for it.

Come near, O Jesus, in this quiet hour, and be our Lord and friend.
> Let the peace of Your presence bring a hush over our hurriedness.
> Let the strength of Your purity put new power in our personalities.
> And let the love of Your own heart make us, with all men, brothers
>   together with You.
> In the Name of Jesus the Saviour, before Whom every knee shall bow
> in Heaven and on Earth in praise, and gladness, and in glory.

Amen.

O Lord Jesus, Who has taken captivity captive, and blasted Death forever,
    tearing the temple's veil in two
    and trampling the cross beneath Your feet,
    and taking as Your spoils the crown of life:
        We give glory unto You! Praise be, for Your victory!

O God, crosses and crowns,
    and dead men rising from the grave,
    seem long ago and far away to us.
    We were never there, and we do not quite understand how it could
        happen.
    What we do know, though, is how awful death is,
    and how subtle and overpowering our own sin is,
    and how much we need someone
    to come and forgive us, someone
    to set us free, someone to give us new life.

And if that's what Your cross means, Lord,
    if that's what Easter's all about, then we want that.
    We could believe in that!
    We could buy a promise like that.
    God, if we could be born again today we would give the world!
    It would be more to us than silver or gold,
    than lands or houses,
    than cars or clubs,
    than success or fame.
New life!
    O Springtime of the soul, after this long dark winter of our discontent,
    a reborn heart and life to move out in hope again,
    to be soldiers in a great battle again,
    to be men under Christ on the march again.
    If that's what You've done on Easter day,
    hear now our cry of thanks, we pray!

The Gates of New Life

O thank You, Lord, for this magnificent morning!
    Thank You for the dawn of this day,
     for the great worship with this company gathered here,
     and for your bidding heart leaning low over all the world today
     to draw men out to walk Your way.

O Christ, be the Lord of life on Viet Nam's battlefields, we pray.
    Restrain the hand of destruction that is cutting down a grim harvest of
        young lives today.
    Draw us closer to the conference table where we can talk of peace.
    Bless our President and all who labor with him in leading the nation.
    Bless every leader of men, that the way they lead may be the Lord's
        way.
    We pray for all who have asked our prayers today—
     for all those unnamed friends who ask the heart of the Church
     to be held out to them.
    We pray for those who have crossed in triumph to the other side of
        life.
    Give us that triumph, too! Give it to this people gathered here
    that we and all the world may know that by the power of Jesus Christ

*   The strife is o'er, the battle done.*
*   The victory of life is won. The song of triumph has begun!*
*   Alleluia!*

    Amen.

O now my God,
    Whose man I am—weak reed, poor risk, frail tree bending, I can see;
    tossed by every wind of doctrine, doubt, despair.
    No giant pine against the sky, no solid oak, deep-rooted, sure,
    secure against the ravages of time, temptation's toll,
    the Devil's roll.
    Phony facsimile of a tree—hollow, empty, weak,
    a man who here must seek only a hand upon the cheek,
    some forgiving word, some redemption—so absurd for all You've heard.

Salvation, Lord, I claim from Thee.
    Weak, undeserving, I make my plea
for me, and for all men like me who have come to see
    who and what they really be.
    Mercy, Lord. For mercy, Lord, I pray
    for me and all my brothers here today—
    that in our sin and worthlessness
    You would come and give us holiness:
        a sure and strong salvation!
    An end to doubt and dark,
    an end to lonely valleys where a shadow walks.
    But hills and home, and sky and sun, and One
    Who is, and was, and will be everyday
    the One sure, only, companion of my way.

O Lord, all hearts look up to Thee. Every soul comes seeking Thee.
    All claim a hope in Thee, and pray by some mysterious heavenly
    alchemy to be set free!
Hear, Lord, our prayer!

We ask for all men, too. The young and brave and true
    who on the far-off fields of battle do what they can do—
    and fight, and die, and wonder why; and hope and pray they're
        serving You.
And those on other battlefields—of faith, where young men's lives are also
       lost
    and victories won by great cost.

And those of patience on a hospital bed, where lonely pain lies red,
and bodies and battles are wed till healing comes.

So many prayers, and such great need, and we so poor to sow such seed!
You give the increase, Lord, and reap the harvest,
and save the souls and heal the lives,
and win the world.
And, if You can, in Your love so grand, *win us.*

Amen.

Gracious and eternal God, Who was in the beginning,
  is now, and ever shall be, world without end;
Universal God, Who binds the Pleiades and looses the bands of Orion;
  Who was there in the drifting distances of space
  when the morning stars sang together,
  and all the sons of God shouted for joy.
Ever present God, Who not only rides the winds of the world
  but also was at yesterday's coffee party,
  and today's church service, and on tomorrow's highways,
  in the loving, living Spirit of Jesus Christ,
  in Whom You chose to enter this world's life and strife,
  and fear and fortune:

We are here at the behest of Jesus. We've heard Him call.
We've felt the power this very hour, and come to give Him all!
We could not stay away,
  for now we know that at the name of Jesus every knee shall bow and

> *every tongue confess Him King of Glory now.*
> *'Twas Your own pleasure, we should call Him Lord,*
> *Who from the beginning was the incarnate Word!*

Glory, Lord, to You' Honor! Blessing! Power! And thanks!
Thanks for Your mercy. Thanks for Your undeserved forgiveness.
Thanks for being where we needed You, all this summer long:
  on the highways, by the lake,
  in the mountains, alone beneath the stars,
  in our work, and in our hearts!

Thanks for bringing us back together. Thanks for giving us the Church,
  and for breaking its heart open, and plowing the fields of our lives,
  and scattering seed in the furrows of our faith,
  and bringing us to this autumn of harvest.
Harvest of souls, Lord. They're all around us, waiting to be reaped.
  We ourselves are waiting, all waiting to be gathered in!
  On this day of days we sense a moving of Your Spirit.

We know You're near, brooding over the face of this people—
over all this village, praying for us, drawing us toward Thee,
stirring our hearts to see if, restless, with Divine discontent,
we might something glorious and Christlike be.
And so, until that day—so near, and dear, when Your Own Spirit will fall,
and Your heart will call everyone, all—
into Your hand, into Your band,
we give You our lives, ourselves, for good and for all the world.

Amen.

O Jesus Christ,
    come down among men from the hills of home.
    Mountain man,
        Who walked God's hills, and from their heights
        saw many a dawn
        and many a sun drop down to night,
        and saw birds in flight,
        and smelled the anemones in the field,
        and loved the earth.
    Village man,
        Who planed rough wood to make it smooth,
        and tempered rough lives to make them gentle,
        and sat with children in the marketplace.
All this You left when Your hour came;
    all this, so loved, You left behind, and came out of the hills
    to the cities of men:
        To their hunger and longing,
        to their eager waiting and despair.
        Hope You gave them, and wondrous love.
        And to You they gave a curse, and a cross.

O Hero from Heaven,
    mighty man of quiet courage,
    Who saw the cross ahead
    and wept over Jerusalem, the faithless city,
        but never turned back,
        never gave in to fear,
        nor forsook Your God,
        nor denied Your destiny:
    Grant to our hearts something of the hero in Your soul.

As we see the cross ahead,
    help us in our hearts to walk this way with You.
    Help us to meet our hour as soldiers of the cross—
    unafraid as our Master was unafraid,
    glad and brave as He was glad and brave,
    and with faith sure and certain
    as His indeed was certain and was sure.

Jesus Our Hero

So chasten and teach our hearts
    through days like these,
    that when the great day comes
    our hearts may burst their tomb, and fill the breeze
    with alleluia songs,
        and hosannas to the Highest!

        Amen.

Gentle and loving Lord,
    Whose hand is a healing hand,
    Whose heart is a winsome heart,
    Whose love is an inviting, magnetic love
        whenever You're there: Across a crowded room,
        on a factory floor,
        in a sales meeting,
        even in a waiting expectant church,
    men see you. And they always come to You—
        to the exciting group that gathers round You
        in conversation at the party,
        to the group that talks with You before the business meeting,
        to the church that seems to have caught Your Spirit and
        seems somehow to even know You.
    Men come because You draw them,
        You do not turn them back.
        They want to see You again.
        They want You as their friend.

O great Friend of all mankind, and our friend,
    hear our prayer as we cry to You.
    We all love You, and want to do and be what You want us to do and be.
    We're not fighting You, Lord. We're with You.
    Your battle to win the world is our battle.
    Your longing to touch, and heal, and draw to Yourself
    the heart of this town is our longing.

We thank You for Your Great Spirit, the Holy Spirit, that is alive in the
        world,
    bringing You into every life and every land that dares to ask for You.

     Come, Holy Spirit, heavenly dove,
      With all Your quickening power,
     Kindle a flame of sacred love,
      In these cold hearts of ours.

Dear God, light up our lives.
　　Make our hearts burn like the watchfires of a hundred circling camps,
　　and let them shine the light from hill to hill
　　with the message that Christ has come,
　　　　that He is here,
　　　　that the King has come,
　　　　and that He welcomes all men home to Him.
　　　　　　Hallelujah!

　　　　Amen.

O God, You must love this people very much!
>You must have a great dream for us, a marvelous plan!
>You must be preparing us for something
because You've given us so much! Such high moments, such great days.
>It's been a great week for us on so many fronts:
>We gather here from mission forums,
>>from Bible study and prayer breakfast groups,
>>from a vacation church school where many children met and
>>received their Lord,
>>from sacred moments when young people were married.
>>And for some, from the portage paths and sunset waters
>>of the land of northern pine and dipping paddle,
>>and from hours alone with the Lord who made it all, we come.

We come here—here to this graceful, gracious meetinghouse we love,
>here among this family of faith whom even more we love—
to thank You for it all.
>To stand before You tall,
>and tell the world we're Yours.
>To tell the world we're glad to be alive,
>>glad to have gone out in Your Name,
>>glad to be men of the cross,
>>glad to claim the name of Christian,
>>and glad to give to You our lives again!

O Jesus, Lord, with great joy we come to hear Your Word to us
>about telling the Good News of God to all the world.
We thank You for an Andrew, who loved the Lord enough to tell his
>brother,
>and so give the world a Peter.
We thank You for those who stand up here to declare they have no
>fear of being comrades in the cause of Christ.
We thank You for every life received, and for every heart sent out
>in Jesus' Name.

Facing Life with Christ

O Lord, may the message of the cross be heard with power in this hour
    in the land of the Prince of Peace,
    and may the jungle guns be silent,
    nor explode there again, nor in the hills, nor anywhere.
Let your peace enfold the world,
    and most especially the hearts
        that in this very hour
        are looking for the right,
        and for the light,
        and for You, Lord, and Your power.

                Amen.

O Lord, the Light that makes bright the night;
   Lord, the dawn that turns the dark to day;
   Lord, Whose Shepherd heart walks out and finds us when we lose the way,
      and Whose eternal watch keeps all of us within Your loving sight:
Mindful are we of the marvelous mystery we see,
      of a Lord Who dies for us while we yet sinners be;
      Who woos us in that magnetic Man, Christ Jesus,
      in Whom is also God in amazing, dying love divine.
We come to You this misty morning
      grateful for the Spirit that draws us here;
      grateful for the love that has made this church our own heart's home;
      and grateful for the power of prayer that's here—
      that even beside us in the pew,
      believing hearts are bent to You.
O God! What a company is the Christian Church!
      What a comradeship of friends is here
      that makes it easy to bow down
      and give up every fear.

We thank You that this is our privilege:
      To be a believing, witnessing, working part of Your Church
         in this hour of decisive history.
      To stand among the saints and sinners of our time,
      the humble-hearted who know their one great need is God the Lord,
         in Jesus Christ.
Lord, our pride we leave at home,
      along with our dreams of grandeur
      and our self-image of power—

         Nothing in our hands we bring,
         Only to Your cross we cling!

Will you take us, Lord?
      Will You let us be committed comrades of the cross with You?
         We want You so much!
         We want You here.
         We want Your holy angels to attend us;

to come trouble the waters of our time,
and pour out power on Your Church which seems so power-
less.
God! We haven't begun to do what You could do through us if we would
only dare.
We haven't begun to be the power we could be, with You.
O Christ, crucify the worldly fear in us that keeps You out—
You can do all things through those who love You!
You can win the world. You can win our town.
From this one little company of people, You can mount a mission
the likes of which we've never seen, nor ever dared believe could
be.
O angel messengers of the living God, break through to us!
Break down our doors. O'ertake our unwilling hearts.
Come, O come, Lord Jesus!

And come to this sin-sick world. Come to lost and bleeding Viet Nam.
Our consciences trouble us, and tell us that death from the air
or death from the marshes and the rice paddies *still is death,*
and we and our country are called to be bringers of life!
Show us the way.
We hold up the President. Steady his heart.
Make him wise. Surround him with our prayers.

Surround the Congress, too, with prayer.
Let them not give up the course of right and justice at home
just because it is no longer politically profitable.
Surround our city with prayer:
our schools,
our political parties,
our hospitals and institutions of mercy.
Surround our missionaries everywhere—
and surround us—
and make us for Your love's sake
a mighty mission for Jesus Christ,
Who is the Way, the Truth, and the Life!
To You, all glory be, O Lord!

Amen. Amen.

Lord of the Upper Room,
> Who on a dark and lonely night twenty centuries ago
> entertained a secret guest, and bid him welcome,
> and told him the truth of life—"Be born again!"
So we, too, come seeking, Lord.
> Looking for the truth in an upper room,
> looking for a Lord Who died for sin and yet Who lives;
> Who was killed by hatred and yet Who loves;
> Who was a poor man and yet Who made our world rich!
O Father in Heaven, help us to see the glory of God in the face of Jesus
>   Christ!
> Help us to see the light when the night is dark.
> Help us to catch the glory in our hearts!

O glory, glory to the Lord, indeed! Hallelujah for a world that's freed!
> Thank You, Lord! Thank You for the Spirit's song!
> Thank You for Your love so strong!
O Redeemer of a whole world's life,
> Who rescues men from the storm and strife—
>> glory to our Christ's great Name
>> glory to our Lord, and all His fame!

O Jesus of Jerusalem,
> Who stormed the city with a heart aflame
> and planted Your cross across its name:
>> We honor the cross, and laugh at the shame,
>> for the world will be won by that great Name!

Plant it in our hearts today, O Christ our King.
> Make it our banner on the way, as this day we sing.
> Triumphant today, all our lives we bring!

We would see Jesus, God.
> We too would knock our knock at the upper room,
> and ask our questions by the light of the moon.
> In the still holy light, with the Table's silver gleaming bright,
> we need it so. On this day we need it so.

O helping and healing Lord,
    we need Your love for families struck down by death today—
    be their help and hope through all the way.
    We need it, too, for those who fight for life in a hospital room.
    And for a whole company who feel the doom
    of a tragic crash that in one great smash
    of the fist of fate wiped out their best, and all help was too late.
O help of the world, hope of a thousand million hearts,
    the light in our dark, the sun in our day,
    great companion along life's torturous way:
    To You be the glory and all the glad songs,
    for this is our story—You right all our life's wrongs!
        Thank You, Christ.
        Thank You, and Amen!

O winds of Heaven, blowing off the western plains,
  sweeping through the morning light of a glad and glistening day;
winds of the western sea from all the blue Pacific,
wind that has whistled down the mountains of the West
  and brings the warming kiss of God
  in summer's blessing to our Earth:
We wait for yet another wind.
We wait for still another sound from Heaven:
  a far-off rushing sound like angel wings against the window,
  like the roar of the jet from a far-off field,
  like the falls of a mighty river rushing to the sea.

We seek the sound of the winds of God.
  We look for the fires of a burning faith.
  We wait for the wonder of the joy of Jesus,
  for the great outcry of the loud "Amen!"
  as the voice of many waters
  and of mighty thunderings saying "Alleluia!
    For the Lord God Omnipotent reigneth!"

We wait, O Lord, for the pouring out of the gift of Your Pentecostal
  Spirit upon all of us, Your people.
  O Lord, we know we are not worthy.
  We know we all have sinned and come short of the glory.
  But we love You, we need You,
  we adore You, we cry out to You.

Save us Lord 'ere we perish!
  Light a new fire in the cold ashes of our faith.
  Give a new life to our worried, weary hearts;
  blow into our beings the winds of God today.
  And make us, we pray, men of Your Spirit.
  Heralds and apostles, Lord, we'd be—
  men with the Gospel trumpet to our lips, and people with a passion,
  and a love, and a care for the lives of men in Christ's great Name.

Use Us in the Task

O Jesus Christ, sweep through the open winds of this meetinghouse!
    Banish away all in it that is false or merely form.
    They count for nothing, Lord—none of the form or pageantry,
    or the clothes, or cars mean anything, Lord.
    Only the hearts bowed here, count, Lord,
    asking for Your blessing, and waiting for Your free Spirit.
        Hear our prayer, O Lord.

And not just for ourselves. For Your churches across our land,
    grant them all Your great Spirit today. And may the spirit of peace
    lie over the battlefields of the world today, and over every cemetery
    where soldiers lie, and heroes rest.
    Comfort all the grieving hearts and all the weary lives, holding close
    to You every burdened soul, as You've held us!
        And alleluia unto the Lamb, Our Lord, Who was, and is,
        and is to come!

        Amen.

O God of the everlasting hills,
 before all this beauty our spirit thrills:
  For an August morning
  that brings a warning
   that summer is on the wane,
   and that with inward pain
 we must turn our highland hearts toward city streets again
 and think of the needs of men—
 their sickness and their sin,
  the world of trouble they're in,
  the ways of woe they've been,
  and their indomitable desire to win!

We must go back, Lord, to the trains and planes,
 the smoke and strains, and the hordes and the whirl
 that are all a part of Your world.
We want to go back. We're ready to go.
 To meet if we can these needs that we know;
 to play our part on the stage of men,
 to answer the call that always comes when
 we are needed as doctors, or lawyers,
 or teachers, or friends,
 or salesmen, or civil servants,
 or statesmen, or just men.

Make us wise, Lord, as we deal
 with the laws of the land
 or the sick that are at hand,
 or with difficult wars we feel are not right
 or all of the agonies that wake us at night.
 —The problems of business and labor—this critical strike,
  Of steel and inflation, and riot and fright.

O Jesus Christ of compassion and care—remember our President
 who always must bear our national burdens, our problems and hopes
 as his personal burden, his challenge to cope.

We thank You he had a proud day of his own
when his daughter was married—and his one thought alone!
We thank You for a Civil Rights law—poor though it may be,
and pray for the day when for justice everywhere there will be victory!
We pray for the men who man the airlines of the land,
and for the critical issue that is in their hand.
And especially Your wisdom and help we ask for our
Christian comrades on both sides of the table.
    Show them a way, Lord.
We pray too, as a brother has asked
for St. Mark's Church, and its deacons as they face the task
of being the church and proclaiming the Christ
in a city in India that needs such a church and needs such a Christ.
We pray for the Church in the world, Lord—everywhere that men gather
    today,
to hear a word from the Lord, then disperse to the world,
to live its truth there:
for the Christian Church in New York, in Washington,
    in Minneapolis and Brooklyn
    in England and America . . .
Make her great, O God—great in city, great in suburb.
Great on college campus, great in office.
Great in factories, great in home.
Great in the marketplace, and on the battlefield over all our world!
And great in our hearts!
O let the Lord Jesus be great in our hearts!
Make us humble enough to love Him,
and live for Him,
and die for Him too,
if He needs our death, for His world to live.

And thank You for a good day, God—
for the sun on these hills of home,
for the peace of this mountain meadow
for asters along the roads and Indian paintbrush on the hills,

for these northern lakes we love
and for this wayside Chapel:
A reminder to country men and city friend alike
that over all the land—
     over field and forest, sea and sand
     and over every man
You are the Lord
     and whether in summer hills
     or winter street
You will be there
     our every need to meet!
     Glory! Hallelujah!

    Amen. Amen.

O Lord of hosts, on this glad day
      I claim Your love to guard my way.
  Christ's hand to hold, His Word to say,
  His faith to lean on when I pray.

Without Your power I'll only fail,
      stand up to speak, then turn and quail!
  Be You my shield, my breastplate strong,
  when by Your Spirit I fight the wrong!

O gracious Christ, my wondrous Friend,
      Who into His world He doth me send:
  Let nothing of myself contend,
  but, free for Thee, my life to spend!

O God my Christ, Who came to me
      and gave the vision that I might see,
  a burning fire let my life be,
  that by my word some might find Thee.

Make me a herald, Lord, the watchman's cry on the city wall,
      a blazing beacon standing tall,
  a voice for You before I fall—
  that to Your Name the world may call.

So let me live, Lord, brave and true;
      with Your great Spirit, me endue.
  And take the life, Lord, I give to You,
  that it may be Christ's, Lord, through and through.

And 'ere we part take in Your love
      the names we speak, to You above.
  Lay healing hands on them, and make them well.
  And those lately widowed, I pray Your comfort and peace to tell.

And God of nations, as well as men,
      hold back from war Your people when
    in fear, to fight, we seem to send
    bullets and planes, others' wills to bend.

And from disaster our friends deliver,
      who so late, in fear, their lives did quiver.
    Make our hands to help, and show the way
    that love can say, "We stand with you, today, today!"

So hear the prayer Your people say,
      that Christ may win the world today,
    and all men find the way, *the way—*
    And our great Christ hold all in sway!

                Amen.

Prayers for the Army of the Lord

O Lord of life, Who never was ashamed to live where we live:
> Who loved the kitchen hearth where Lazarus and his sisters lived,
> Who stood alone with a woman taken in adultery,
> Who sat down and ate in Zaccheus' house;
> Who was not afraid of priest or peasant, brothel or bar,
> but who went wherever a man in darkness looked for light,
> and held out the hand whenever a man stumbled and reached out to
> > take it.

O Christ Who cares,
> Who will go to the ends of the Earth to redeem a lost life,
> Who will watch for hours by the bed of the sick,
> Who will stand strong with the man who is weak or has failed,
> Who is humble enough to make time for a child:

We thank You that You see so much of good in us,
and that each little child is the promise of a whole life to You.

Lord, there is so much that we can be.
> Even when we have failed, or lost our way,
> You can do anything with our lives.
> With You nothing is impossible. With You no door is closed to us,
> > no way barred, no opportunity forbidden.
> Our lives can go as far as we will let You take them.
> Our hopes can reach as high as any heart that sees the sky.
> Our strength can be as strong as any great faith can make it.

Lord God, we have such potentialities as a people!
> Deep in the heart of each one here there is such love,
> and power, and sheer hunger for the highest.
> We could break the heart of evil!
> We could draw the sting of sin!
> We could destroy the dragon of despair—
> with Your love in our hearts, with Your power in our personalities!

For Skill with the Weapons

O mighty God, help us to see what a people of power You have made us.
Help us to see across the world the whole battlefield of life,
where our love and power could turn the tide
of apathy and indifference and evil
into a wave of the future for courage and honesty and love!

We pray for our city and its leaders in every realm of life,
that despite the perils of prosperity
the courage of great conviction may characterize us always.
In the Name of the One Who makes all things possible—
Jesus Christ.

Amen.

Spirit of God,
>   Watchman upon the ramparts of Everyman's soul—
>   Who sees the night fall and the dawn come;
>   Who watches through all the long hours when our spirits sleep,
>   straining through the darkness of life to see any sin approaching
>   or evil lying in wait:
>   You are the One Who stirs our consciences awake in danger's hour,
>   Who sounds the alarm until the sleeping city of our soul stirs from
>   slumber and our consciences rise to battle.

O Guardian of our lives, gratefully we sound our thanksgiving to You!
>   For all the lonely hours of life when the tide of battle seemed so
>   surely to have turned against us, and suddenly the night was lit
>   with the light of angel hosts riding to our rescue;
>   for moments when temptation had all but bound us hand and foot,
>   and the strength of Your Spirit came in wondrous ways to set us
>   free!

Surely You have been the whole armor of God to Christian men in every
>   generation,
>   enabling them to stand against all the wiles of the devil—
>   making Peter to stand as a mighty rock in a weary land,
>   making of Paul a proud trumpet to call the cohorts of Christ to the
>   cause,
>   making the restless soul of an Augustine to fling away the lusts
>   of life and to find its rest in You,
>   making all the great names of the faith—
>   Benedict and Bernard, Luther and Hus, Livingstone and
>   Schweitzer—
>   to be strong in the Lord.

O mighty Spirit of our Lord and Saviour, be our armor we pray—
>   for it is not against other men that we wrestle,
>   not against the forces without but against the forces within,
>   against the whole kingdom of evil:
>   against principalities, against powers,
>   against the rulers of the darkness of this world,
>   against spiritual wickedness within the high and holy places of our
>   own hearts!

Arm us, O God, that we may be able to withstand in the evil day.
> Wrap us round with truth. Give dishonesty no place in our souls.
> Fasten on us the breastplate of righteousness, that not all the
>> hosts of evil together may ever defeat us, nor shred our allegiance
>> from any one of us!

O Lord Jesus, whatsoever things are true, whatsoever things are just,
> whatsoever things are pure, whatsoever things are lovely, whatsoever
>> things are of good report:
>> If there be any virtue or any praise, help us think on these things.

And we ask this for all our brethren in the Lord, for every child of Yours
> among us, or anywhere on the Earth:
> Stand near the tempted and the weak, forgive us all our shortcomings,
> heal the sin we know so well, redeem the sorrowing from their grief,
>> the lonely from their solitude, the troubled from their burdens,
>> the sick from their weakness, and the dying from their pain.
> Forget not our brothers in the battle who are daily in our hearts,
>> for we remember them still.
> In Christ's strong Name—our hero and our help—we ask this.

Amen.

All-seeing and all-knowing God,
    have You gathered us here for some special purpose?
    Do You have orders for us, some work to do,
        some cause to serve?
    If the army You want us to enter is the Lord's,
    and if the banner we are to fight under is the cross,
        enlist our lives today!

Don't let us be afraid or hold back at fear of losing worldly things.
    Don't let us ever shrink from signing up in Your Book above,
    deeding all we are and all we have
        to our commander Christ, and to His cause.

O make us worthy soldiers on the battlefields of life:
    Snipers, guerillas, battalionmen in columns
    who look everywhere—in office, shop,
        at parties, and at home—for lives to capture
        and commit to Christ.

Make us skillful soldiers with Heaven's arsenal of weapons:
    the Bible, full of truth;
    and Prayer, the greatest weapon any Christian has.
    Make us people of prayer, who knock on Heaven's door
        for those who need a friend but have not found the greatest
            Friend of all.
        For the unknown thousands who mourn for one they love;
        for those who, if life be saved, must spend long weeks in hospital.
        For those who in body or mind are sick, yet carry on.
        For those who pray in God's house, but do not yet love God's
            children.
        For those who made vows to God but now forget them.
        For all manner of men and women we offer prayer, O Lord.

And God, Who signs up even sinners into the ranks of the faithful:
    Sign me up, enlist me—the greatest of all sinners—
    into Your company, where there is the forgiveness of the family of faith,
        and Your love. In Jesus' Name.

Amen.

Great God! Who made a world that gave to man the best of everything,
    and set in his heart a dream to be the best that he could be:
    What a wonderful thing is a Minnesota morning in winter,
    with the snow white and the sun bright.
    And what beautiful perfection there is, Lord, in a stand of pine,
        and in white birches along the sky-blue waters
        of a northern lake in summer.
    God, thank you! For the scampering fun of a little rabbit,
        for the perfect balance of a robin's wing,
        for the lavender loveliness of the lilacs in the spring:
            Bless You, Lord, for everything—
                perfect, whole, and ingeniously made
                by the Creator Craftsman's hand.

And God, what a wonderful thing is man, and all you have made in him.
    For his striving for the highest, best, the good and right.
    For his body of beauty:
    For the muscles of a man, for the sprinter in the blocks
        poised and strained to explode into speed,
    for a skier slanting gracefully down the hill with his
        body arched in a comma of moving grace;
    for the opera star's marvelous high "C" singing out over
        a great hall filled with people in wondrous awe,
    for a politician crying out great words that hold a people spellbound;
    for a boy in a swimming meet splashing down the lane with all he has,
        to do his best;
    for a policeman directing traffic with that assured perfection
        that suggests a sense of fun;
    for a salesman's day when every account is there, and needs what
        he has to sell;
    for a schoolteacher on the day she makes sense to a boy in her class,
        and gets to his heart as well as his head, and he learns the truth—
            these are such good things, God!

Help us to love the good!
    Help us stand for the true!
    Help us appreciate the beautiful, and let us do nothing to make us less
    than our best.

Don't let us eat too much, or smoke too much, or sit around and waste
      our lives.
Don't let us dull our minds, or weaken our will, or compromise our
      character
        through the hollow laughter of the cocktail party,
        and the moments lost with the martini.

For a whole mind, and a clear eye, and a strong body that is the temple of
      the soul,
      we thank You, Lord!
We're glad it's a world moving too fast for anything unworthy to catch up,
      a world that needs just the best:
      The best minds, the best bodies, the best spirits, the best men.
      Men fit to be soldiers of the King, the great King, Who makes soldiers
        of all men who are ready to be their best for Him.
Thank You for the gift of the best to all Your children, for whom we pray to
      You now—
      that they and we may be made whole, and clean, and fresh, and new
        in Jesus Christ, the Lord, our King.

Amen.

O God, so many men are Yours! And yet we stand before the staggering
    immensities of the city and the world and cry out, despairing:
    "But who are we among so many?"

And yet You answer: "I have five thousand men in this city who have
    not bowed the knee to Baal." Five thousand who stand up for
    You, five thousand who fight for You.

Your men are five thousand times five thousand!
    So many men are Yours. We shake our heads, doubting,
    and yet we could stand among the best of the world, believing!
    We are afraid to do anything,
    and yet we could stand among the finest, fighting!

O God, Who has many men on Your side today—
    great men, good men, wise men, well-known men:
    Show us the glorious company in which we stand,
    show us the valor of the victorious, show us the bravery of the best,
    show us the love of the little-known.

O Great God, Who has touched with Your love all manner of men,
    we stand among a host! We are an army—we men who believe—and
    on every corner stands our company!
    In every city are our soldiers—we can win the world!

Make us march, O God. Line us up for battle!
    Fashion us for the fight! Show us our cause is right!
    And then, with hearts aflame and lives triumphantly the same,
    and battles to be won for the Name of Jesus Christ,
    send us out—Your emissaries in this world,
    to tell of love and truth, with flag unfurled!
    And let Your flag fly over us this week,
        and over the ones we love—"Love's banner floating o'er them"—
        and over every life where love's banner can be,
        the bond to bind us close to Christ the King,
            our comrade and our commander!

                        Amen.

For Courage in the Fight

O Great God, Whose Spirit broods over our waiting November world,
    and Who, in Jesus Christ, the Master of men,
    has sent out a sower to sow,
    and has planted in our lives such deep desires that our
    hearts are restless until they rest in You:

Glory do we give to You, praise and honor sing we to Your Name,
    Who has furrowed the fields of our hearts,
    and sown the seed of the Word in our lives,
    and has hoed and watered and nurtured us
    until that day when we shall bring forth good fruit, and the whole
    Earth may be fed by the bread of life broken open by the life of
    Christ, lived in our hearts!

We believe, O Lord, that the fields are white with harvest!
We believe, O Christ our Saviour,
    that lives on every hand are waiting to be gathered in,
    waiting to hear the call of Christ, waiting to see the hand outstretched
        to them.
    Waiting to hear the distant triumph song
    of the servants and soldiers of the Saviour coming over the hills
    to greet them, and welcome them, and to call them to be part of the
    pilgrim band, the wayfarers in the world, journeymen for Jesus,
    Strangers and sojourners in the Earth—winning the world for the Lord!

O Jesus, Lord, gather close our every brother and sister
    and friend and fellow Christian, and make them Yours today!
    Let no child of Yours escape this place today,
    without at least the knowledge that here he has met the Master,
        that here he has caught the vision,
        that here has been a true people of God,
        a great company of Christians.

And, O Lord, on such a day as this,
    send us back into the highways and byways of the world
    as living witnesses to the compassion of Christ for all the world:

For every truck driver and cabby, every carpenter and counselor,
every teacher and tradesman, every salesman and executive of this city—
until metropolis comes to know the light of the Lord shining in its midst,
until we and all who walk with us become the world's light the Lord sent us
    to be.
Light the fires of the Spirit, O Lord, today.
Make of our nation a light to all peoples.
Let Your Light shine in our President, and senators, and governors.
Let it shine as a healing hand across those blasted and gutted
    battlefields of Viet Nam,
and let the lives of the men of Christ be for the healing of the nations.

Amen. Amen.

O God,

> *For all the saints, who from their labors rest,*
> *Who Thee by faith before the world confessed,*
> *Thy Name, O Jesus, be forever blest. Alleluia!*
> *O may Thy soldiers, faithful, true, and bold,*
> *Fight as the saints who nobly fought of old,*
> *And win, with them, the victor's crown of gold. Alleluia!*

O Captain in the well-fought fight,
>Who in the darkness is our only light,
>with Your strong hand give us Your might!

We love You, Lord, We want to be Yours.
>We want to be Your army,
>Your troops with Heaven for home, Your expeditionary force
>with no purpose in the world but to do Your will,
>>to carry out Your orders, to destroy the depots of the Devil,
>and to raise the flag of faith on every battlefield and in every heart!

Help us to be true to the cause, O great Christ, our Commander,
>our Comrade-in-arms, and our companion in the conflict.
>Make Your Church a mission, Lord, and let our returning
>>to headquarters each Sabbath day bring a mission accomplished to
>>report.
>Make us brave in every battle, pure and at peace in heart,
>>and loyal to our Lord.

Make it so even for this church, Lord. Make us a church on the move—
>a joyful, confident, victorious church;
>a singing, swinging, smiling, laugh-filled church.
>A church where new Christians are made every day,
>where weary hearts find hope, where lonely lives meet the Great Friend,
>where the world can be healed and helped.

Bless the whole Church in our town—every congregation.
>They're all Yours, Lord. We're your troops. Send us out together!

For Loyalty to the Commander

And Lord, hold close to You those who fight on
    fields of blood and battle,
    where swords are not yet beaten into plowshares,
    nor spears into pruning hooks.
        Heal them, Lord, and us. In the strong Name of Jesus Christ.

                                   Amen.

O Jesus, Master from the mountainside,
    rebel leader who called the nation back to God,
    strange patriot, commander of the hearts of men,
    Who on this day comes down from the hills with Your guerilla band
    to take the capital city with one stroke of Your uplifted hand:
    We hail You! Hosanna to the Son of David.
    Blessed is He that cometh in the Name of the Lord!

O Christ, crowned by the Sabbath sunlight of this triumphal day in spring,
    moving like a conqueror through Your crowds—loving them,
    welcoming them, blessing them
    even while You know that some of them will turn tail in the time of
            trial,
    that they won't all stand by, that there are betrayers in the crowd,
    and that they are a crowd following where others lead,
    moved by a mass mind, sheep without a shepherd.

O Lord, Who turns no man from You—not even fickle men, or confused men,
    or simply curious men—but Who receives them all,
    Who welcomes any man Who will walk Your way:
    Let us be in Your crowds today. We know what is ahead.
    We know about the upper room, about Calvary and that awful cross.
    Give us a chance, Lord! Let us try again:
        Try to be true, try to be trusting,
        try to be tolerant, try to take up our cross and follow You.

Into the dark we follow You, Lord; into the week that was,
    the week that is now, and will ever be.
    The flickering shadows of the upper room,
    the rolling storm of thunder and wrath sweeping across Calvary's
            cross-crowned hill,
    and finally the day, the dawn, and the triumph song!
        Let us follow You, Lord!

O conquering Christ, before Whom even death finally went down:
    Walk the marshes of the Mekong Delta, and the battlelines of the bush
            country,
    and hold back the hand of death in that wracked and riddled land.

We know there will be wars, and rumors of wars,
    but You also called the nations to beat their swords
    into plowshares, and their spears into pruning hooks.
    Hear our plea for peace!
And hear our plea for peace in the heart and healing of the body for the
    dear ones of this company who are sick in hospital beds.
    Thanks for all things, Good God, Great King,
    Whom now we praise with heart, and life, and everything.
        Hosanna!

        Amen.

O winds of God that blow from the south and make the spring to come.
> Winds of God that blow through the land, and stir the stubble
> of the fields to life, and all the world to life.
O winds of God that blow through the weary winter bodies of our beings,
> and through our burdened brains and sagging spirits:
Praise Be! For on this day we see, that

> > *Lo, the winter is past, the rain is over and gone;*
> *The flowers appear on the earth;*
> > *The time of the singing of birds is come,*
> *And the voice of the turtle is heard in our land.*

O winds of God that bring not only the spring,
> blow through our hearts today!
Winds of God that fan the land into flaming fire,
> blow and glow in our lives till we burn for You, with desire!

O Christ the King, Who disappointed men who came to sing
> two thousand years ago Your praise and wanted so to walk Your ways:
> If you would lead the horde, and rule the world with sceptre and with
> > sword—

Come into Your kingdom today, and make us Your soldiers to stay,
> with weapons of faith for the fray!
O Jesus, Who comes so humbly and yet with such a majesty,
it is with shame and sorrow that we sing the music of this day,
> even while we already hear another sound from a hill far away.
We would like to think we would go with You all the way—
> that never would we fail or falter,
> never disappear when night comes near,
> never leave Your side and run and hide,
> or be the men who turned and lied
> when Christ was captured there, and crucified.

O Forgive us, Lord. We want to be Your men.
We want to be the faithful ones, and true.
> Help us. Help us to see our shame and name Your Name.
> Some of us have never done it.

Some of us have never let You take over.
Some of us have never really said:
   "Come to our hearts, Lord Jesus."
O Christ, come today. Come here. Blow here with Your winds of the Spirit.
   Touch all the hearts with faith's fire.

And hold our weary world in Your hand today.
   Hold Viet Nam there. Hold Africa there. Hold Great Britain there.
   Hold the railroad unions there. Hold Washington there.
   Hold Minneapolis there. Hold the churches there.
   And hold us there.
      In Christ's great and winning Name.

                    Amen.

Lord God, We come into Your house on faltering feet,
> remembering the shining armor of hope and new resolve
> with which we went forth from this house on the Lord's day last—
> ready to do battle with all the forces of evil
>> in the Name of our dear Christ.
> And now we remember how, with each passing day,
>> that armor tarnished—
>> how the stain of weakness, and selfishness, and compromise
>> dulled its brilliance,
> until now we come back to the stronghold of the Lord
>> not as happy warriors, victorious in the cause,
> but as a shame-faced remnant,
>> well-nigh defeated in the battle.
O God, Whose wrath is turned back by the penitents' cry,
> Whose joy is in forgiving the sinners who return,
>> forgive us, we pray.

Bless us with courage to see ourselves, to know wherein we have
> not walked with Jesus;
> to remember when, out there in the world,
> we cried with Peter, "I know not the man!"
And remind us, Lord, that Your call
> is not only to the closet of prayer
> but to the marketplaces of life,
> where many have not heard the Master's call,
> and where men need the Word of Christian love.
Help us to speak where it is not easy to speak.
> Help us to act when we may be criticized for acting.
> Help us to trust that in the day of Jesus Christ
>> the kingdom will finally come.

O remember the poor and those without justice.
> Remember the sick and the social outcasts,
> remember the broken-hearted,
> remember the lonely who look for Jesus to be their friend,
> remember the burdened who long to leave their burdens here.

For Victory in the Battle

And by giving us hearts of compassion and spirits of courage,
   to love the unloved and the lost, who are the Master's friends,
make us His men.
      And let the armor shine,
     and the shield be strong,
     and the sword strike true, for You.

             Amen.

O Great God,
    what a privilege to do service in the cohorts of Christ!
    What high service to be chosen for the ranks of the Galilean!
        To start out each day with Him;
        to walk out upon the hills of life in the sudden splendor
            of the morning sun;
        to labor, and love, and lift through the long day with
            His hand helping;
        to fight life's great battles with His shouts of command
            and encouragement
            carrying across the dust and turmoil of the day.
    And at last, when evening comes,
    and the campfires are lit,
    and the troops come home
        weary with the long day's warfare,
    that word of peace across the camp—
        "Well done, good and faithful servant!"

O Lord, what life in all the world
    could begin to touch this life we have with Christ?
What thrill could be ever greater
    than to lift His banner above the battle
    and see His love going on before, to conquer all?

So make us a mighty host,
    ready to move out to do the deeds of soldiers and of heroes.
    Make us Yours.
    And make Christ count so much to us
    that nothing would we not sacrifice for Him—
        even life, and fortune, and our sacred honor.
            So on to victory, Lord,
            through Christ our Conqueror and King!

                    Amen.

O Lord, Who has called us from the fishing nets of life
    to take up our cross and follow You;
    to leave the petty and mundane,
    the daily and the drab,
    to set off into the sun;
    up onto the hills of life
    where the sky is blue,
    and the wind blows free,
    and there to walk with Thee,
    to march with exulting song,
    like a mighty army all our life long;
    living, witnessing, and shining like a beckoning beacon
    in the world, as Your Church:

Deliver us from all the things of self,
    whether pride or wealth,
    that hold us back—
        that blacken the beam,
        that turn our light into night,
        that chain down our freedom,
        that drown out our song,
        that make our faces long,
    that in any way make our witness
    a black mark upon the golden glory of the cross!

Set us on our way again, O Christ.
    Let the old songs swell once more;
    let our message and mission be bright, not a bore;
    and let Your Church most truly be,
    for all who have eyes to see,
    the chariot of the Gospel!
Glory, Lord! Glory be to You! Amen and Alleluia!

And Lord Jesus,
    draw close to the heart of God each one of us—
    where, in wonder, love, and praise,
    and without shadow of doubt or pursuit of pride,
       we can be His—all His.

       Amen. Amen.

May the roads rise for you,
May the winds be always at your back,
And may the Lord hold you
In the hollow of His hand.

An Alphabetical Index of the Prayers